The 'Occult' Experience and the New Criticism

The 'Occult' Experience and the New Criticism

Daemonism, Sexuality and the Hidden in Literature

Clive Bloom
Lecturer in English
Middlesex Polytechnic

HARVESTER PRESS · SUSSEX
BARNES & NOBLE BOOKS · NEW JERSEY

First published in Great Britain in 1986 by
THE HARVESTER PRESS LTD
Publisher: John Spiers
16 Ship Street, Brighton, Sussex
and in the USA in 1987 by
BARNES & NOBLE BOOKS
81 Adams Drive, Totowa, New Jersey 07512

British Library Cataloguing in Publication Data
Bloom, Clive
    The 'occult' experience and the new
    criticism: daemonism, sexuality and
    the hidden in literature.
    1. Literature—History and criticism
    I. Title
    809   PN81
    ISBN 0–7108–0617–5

Library of Congress Cataloging in Publication Data
Bloom, Clive.
    The 'occult' experience and the new criticism.
    1. English literature—History and criticism.
2. Occultism in literature. 3. Literature and
spiritualism. 4. Psychoanalysis and literature.
5. American literature—History and criticism.
6. Literature—Philosophy. I. Title.
PR409.028B55   1987   820'.9'37   86–10963
ISBN 0–389–20646–6

Typeset in Garamond 11/12pt by Witwell Ltd
Printed in Great Britain by
Biddles Ltd, Guildford and King's Lynn

THE HARVESTER PRESS PUBLISHING GROUP
The Harvester Group comprises Harvester Press Ltd (chiefly
publishing literature, fiction, philosophy, psychology, and science and
trade books); Harvester Press Microform Publications Ltd (publishing
in microform previously unpublished archives, scarce printed sources,
and indexes to these collections); Wheatsheaf Books Ltd (chiefly
publishing in economics, international politics, sociology, women's
studies and related social sciences).

For Lesley, James and Jonathan

Odin's *Runes* were the first form of the work of a Hero; *Books* ... are still miraculous *Runes*.... No magic, *Rune* is stronger than a Book. All that Mankind has done, thought, gained or been: it is lying as in magic preservation in the pages of Books.... Literature ... is an 'apocalypse of Nature' a revealing of the 'open secret'.

Thomas Carlyle:
On Heroes and Hero Worship

List of Contents

Preface

Since the advent of structuralism and post-structuralism the conceptual system of traditional literary theory and practice has been consistently attacked as based upon reductionist, metaphoric, metaphysical and theological premises which the structuralists accused the traditionalists of taking, not as fictitious constructs, but as realities. While traditionalists stressed a unified and harmonious meaning to texts radiating from and returning to a textual core (author, theme, etc.,) structuralists and post-structuralists insisted on fragmentation and the absence of centrality. For (post) structuralists traditional criticism in its insistence on the notion of 'truth' and of 'meaning' stresses the linguistic concept of the 'signified' while (post) structuralism in its insistence on codes, practices and textuality stresses the linguistic concept of the 'signifier'. Moreover, while (post) structuralism concerns itself with the construction of the individual (his or her sexuality, psyche, body) through linguistic practice traditional criticism concerns itself with the construction of the individual from an extra-linguistic standpoint. Finally, and most importantly, (post) structuralism centres upon the interactive nature of text and reader (it understands 'transference') while it ignores traditional concerns with the nature of art and the problems of creativity and artistic individuality.

This book is concerned with recuperating and reconsidering certain traditional concepts of textuality through the 'new'

concerns and using the 'new' analytic concepts and tools of (post)
structuralism. It explores the relationship between the polarities
signifier and signified (which Saussure represented as a single
drawn line) in an attempt to redefine the Saussurian model and in
so doing redefine the relationship between the linguistic and the
extra-linguistic dimensions of textuality, redefine the relationship
between text, psyche, sexuality and knowledge and finally
reconsider the notions of analysis, creativity and textuality. To do
this it is necessary to invoke (post) structuralist critical practice in
order to define, by using its own concepts, what conditions its
relationship to textuality and psyche and also to analyse that of
which it cannot speak: its unconscious (just as [post] structuralism
sees itself as the unconscious of traditional criticism). In order to
consider that 'unconscious' it was necessary to look for certain
'occulted' (or hidden) themes, practices and relationships between
texts and readers and between the act of analysis and the object of
analysis and to consider the notion of the daemonic (or hidden
compulsion) that defines textuality and textual practice but is
itself extra-linguistic. Through this method, which sees (post)
structuralism as a form of modernist creativity and not simply as
theory, I have tried to produce a syncretic approach which
includes, and reconciles, the two sides of Saussure's sign in a
dynamic model which, while centred on the individual subject, is
removed from simple reductionist traditionalism. Indeed I have
tried to define a metaphysics of the text (metaphor as action, the
Word and sexuality, sexuality, text and knowledge) in a rigorous
synthesis of theory *in* practice.

1

The Grammar of Generation and the Mark of Self-Making

A short analysis of the grammatical mark in the poetry of John Donne, Shakespeare and Emily Dickinson

A poetry of sexual alchemy is a poetry of hesitation, union and regeneration; it finds its meaning not overtly, but covertly in an unresolved ambiguity of gender imagery which unites but does not define. The principle of such poetry is one, not of mere figurativeness, but of a figurativeness which has the power to alter the real in terms of itself—bending reality and reshaping it to the point where it participates in the process of figuration, of linguistically 'bodying' forth. The transcendent terms of this 'bodying' forth dealt with in erotic imagery find reverberations in the sexuality of the reader's psyche in which the archetypes of androgyny and bisexuality survive darkly. Yet, this transcendence is not resolved, for in attempting to unite male and female principles in an ideally eroticised union (in which the dual principles of the self are finally resolved as one) this poetry must employ a fundamental and unresolvable antithesis in language—male and female can only unite in the space between their invocation or in the grammatical mark which defines that division. In Donne's *The Flea* the eroticism of blood is imagined through the love-vampirism of a common parasite[1]. And yet this parasite is itself the very emblem of a biologically syntactic union between the images of maleness (the 'I' of the poem) and that of femininity (the 'temple' and 'honour'). To turn the first person singular and the second person singular into a third person plural a mark is needed both of breakage and of union, both of sacrifice and repair:

Oh stay, three lives in one Flea spare,
Where we almost, nay more than married are.
This Flea is you and I, and this
Our marriage bed, and marriage temple is;
Though parents grudge, and you, we'are met,
And cloistered in these living walls of jet.
Though use make you apt to kill me,
Let not to this, self murder added be,
And sacrilege, three sins in killing three.

Donne's 'flea', as an emblem of union, makes the mark that binds 'honour' to 'blood' and eroticism through a male restitution of honour for loss of chastity (honour). It thereby restores the honour of marriage. The flea assails honour by taking the blood of man and mixing it into the blood of woman. This 'one blood made of two' takes us into the terms of sperm meeting egg and a third term, the flea itself. Sexual intercourse and fertilisation take place outside either body within the space of a relational mark and this mark, which wriggles through the poem, exists not as an image proper but as a grammatical condition. Through the flea maleness and femaleness gain significance:

Mark but this flea, and mark in this,
How little that which thou deny'st me is;
Me it sucked first, and now sucks thee,
And in this flea, our two bloods mingled be.

This grammatical mark, which accomplishes breakage and union, which splits yet unites, which gives significance and relationship is represented visually rather than verbally in the space occupied by the 'comma'. Between 'mark but this flea' and 'mark in this' the graffito sign of the flea makes its appearance, enclosing, delineating, uniting. In the space between that which is male and that which is female the comma(n) 'flea' sets relationships up not within content but containing content as a representative of form. Form itself unites principles of masculinity and femininity beyond the range of its contents. Invisibly to most readers the comma of *The Flea* recognises difference and reconciles difference acting without and beyond

2

speech. A mark of the original 'pneuma' (the breathing pause) and expression, the comma is itself silent, a sign of a noise that is absent; a transcendent term which cannot speak. The comma is the affirmation of a 'life', of the blood-filled flea which accomplishes what the sterility and potential inability of the poetic 'I' cannot achieve: the assault upon and restitution of honour. Here content is a never-achieved life while form actually becomes that life.

In Donne, the sexuality of the grammatical mark takes us beyond the titillation of illicit sexual imagery while it points away from itself to the very imagery it unites *and* denies. It affirms life in the face of a frozen potentiality which itself becomes 'death'. Turning to Shakespeare's *Sonnet XX* we find, in more obvious form, the affirmation and denial of the grammatical mark. I give the well known poem in full:

> A woman's face with Nature's own hand painted
> Hast thou, the master-mistress of my passion
> A woman's gentle heart, but not acquainted
> With shifting change, as is false women's fashion;
> An eye more bright than theirs, less false in rolling,
> Gilding the object whereupon it gazeth;
> A man in hue all hues in his controlling,
> Which steals men's eyes and women's souls amazeth.
> And for a woman wert thou first created;
> Till Nature, as she wrought thee, fell a-doting,
> And by addition me of thee defeated,
> By adding one thing to my purpose nothing.
> > But since she prick'd thee out for women's pleasure,
> > Mine be thy love, and thy love's use their treasure.[2]

Here the grammatical mark is more obvious. The sign of unification, the hyphen between 'master' and 'mistress' immediately invokes a strange paradox in the imagery, an unresolved duality of imagination is required, a type of united parallelism, which is to say that we need to answer one paradox with another. The hyphen finds its own power to unite the terms as a positive mark: it bonds the terms. Nevertheless, at the same time, it pulls those terms apart rendering them unstable, distanced, distinct. Furthermore, such distinction is wrought by a sign that itself represents a mathematical taking away, a denial of the unity it appears to have produced. Neither 'master' nor 'mistress' stand on their own: like the components of Saussure's sign they exist as abstractions united by a minus sign into positive meaning. Saussure's attack on the non-existence of positive signs in language construction seems fulfilled by this prophetic mark.

Indeed, through this mark, and despite its negative and self-contradictory nature, the poem takes shape. I say through this mark and around this mark precisely because the poem starts at this mark: a mark which represents the unresolvable nature of the sonnet's language; neither this nor this, the poem is always 'elsewhere' to its 'single' explanation; as such one can only write 'about' this poem and not 'explain' it.

Taking shape through this negative term which is used to unite and resolve the enigmatic relationship of maleness and femininity, the poem cannot become other than ambiguous, an ambiguity far more disturbing to the reader who asks 'what does it mean?' than the more obviously disturbing sexual titillation of androgyny or homosexuality.

This mark sets meaning—sexual, biographical, biological, historical—aside. Through the formal properties of the sonnet and its imagery sexual parallelism is united via paradox. The image conjured up is that of a daemon, neither male nor female but uniting both, a presence endowed with divine sexuality and the seeming potential of both sexes. Indeed, here is a 'woman's face' united to a 'woman's gentle heart' and yet a 'man in hue'. Together, these attributes allow the daemon to 'steal men's eyes and women's souls amazeth'. Hence, the daemon creates a space between masculinity and femininity which captures both the gaze of mortal men and the souls of mortal women. Mortal men are made blind and mortal women find their souls 'amazed' (groping, if we pun, in a *maze* of blind alleys). Thus, the daemon removes the possibility of vision, robs men and women of sight, of the ability to interpret which sex is appropriate. The daemon takes up its place in the space of an indecision, of an ellipsis, a space marked by the hyphenated phrase we have already noticed. To see the phrase is to be aware of the daemon but *not* to see its presence, for the image of his presence is shrouded and eclipsed

4

by self-contradictory imagery. The 'eye more bright' of the daemon sees mortal sexual longing but chameleon-like has 'all hues in its controlling'.

At the mid-point of the sonnet the daemon momentarily materialises and the poet addresses the moment of its genesis 'and' tells us 'for a woman wert thou first created'. But the materialisation becomes chimaerical, as 'Nature' itself, blinded by its creature falls 'a-doting' and in so doing begins the process of a mad mathematics of addition through negative propositions, in which, 'by addition me of thee defeated'. Addition: 'me + (plus) thee, is invoked through defeat: 'me – (minus) thee, which returns us to the hyphenated 'master-mistress'. The positive sign of masculinity, the daemon's penis apears briefly via implied homosexual union, 'by adding one thing to my purpose nothing' which carries us forward to the pun 'prick'd' later on.

However, this union is conceived but not conceiving, it is mis-union, in which one penis added to another offers no possibility of 'conception'. The speaking 'I' finds 'one thing' represented as 'nothing'. Moreover, even the ghostly male appendage vanishes when the metaphoric conditioning of 'prick'd' is quite obviously absent from this line which ends on 'nothing'.

The 'daemon' which Shakespeare creates in his poem, which takes over the poem and adds nothing to the 'I' that 'speaks' it into being finds itself unable ultimately to choose a definite destiny. Resolved as a male, 'prick'd out for women's pleasure', the daemon loses his 'penis', endowed now, not with a specific masculine sexuality but with a euphemistic 'love' 'treasure[d]' by women. Thus, the daemon will retrieve his 'love' or his penis in the storage house of 'treasure': the female genitalia, a place 'large and spacious' (CXXXV) in which to 'hide' one's 'will'. The resolution to this problem is presented later in Sonnet CXXXV where positive terms finally unite 'Will' to 'will', for 'thou', says the poet, 'being rich in Will, add to thy Will'.

But Sonnet CXXXV has lost its sense of paradox and enigma in the imagery of carnal delight rendering the daemon finally as the mere poet and the poet as a merely mortal lover. Such positive terminology returns the poetry earthward and disavows the divine drive to a transcendent resolution in the uniting of positive terms via a negative and paradoxical mark.

We have, so far, followed the poetry of generation and of duality which unites outside semantics in an external presence beyond the speaker or his subject and which is conditioned by the existence of an 'unacknowledged' grammatical mark in the text. In turning to a poem by Emily Dickinson we again see the progress of a generative mark but this time of a *re-generative* mark uniting not outside of the speaker but within the speaker herself, becoming the very presence that holds together the paradox of a greater femininity spoken of in masculine terms. She writes in poem no. *508*:

> I'm ceded—I've stopped being Theirs—
> The name They dropped upon my face
> With water, in the country church
> Is finished using, now,
> And They can put it with my Dolls,
> My childhood, and the string of spools,
> I've finished threading—too—
>
> Baptized before, without the choice,
> But this time, consciously, of Grace—
> Unto supremest name—
> Called to my Full—The Crescent dropped—
> Existence's whole Arc, filled up,
> With one small Diadem.
>
> My second Rank—too small the first—
> Crowned—Crowing—on my Father's breast—
> A half unconscious Queen—
> But this time—Adequate—Erect—
> With Will to choose, or to reject—
> And I choose, just a Crown—

Upon this poem Adrienne Rich comments, by way of précis:

> Now, this poem partakes of the imagery of being 'twice-born' or, in Christian liturgy, 'confirmed'—and if this poem had been written by Christina Rossetti I would be inclined to give more weight to a theological reading. But it was written by Emily Dickinson, who used the Christian

6

metaphor far more than she let it use her. This is a poem of great pride—not pridefulness, but *self*-confirmation—and it is curious how little Dickinson's critics, perhaps misled by her diminutives, have recognized the will and pride in her poetry. It is a poem of movement from childhood to womanhood, of transcending the patriarchal condition of bearing her father's name and 'crowing—on my Father's breast—.' She is now a conscious Queen 'Adequate—Erect/With Will to choose, or to reject—.'[3]

Rich recognises that here in this poem, as elsewhere in Emily Dickinson's work, the authoress is 'forced' to represent her essential femininity (or proto-feminist womanliness) through a male daemonic presence. However, this persona, argues Adrienne Rich, is not a lost lover in the authoress' biography but a schizoid recognition of a male otherness in her personality *through which* Dickinson's femininity is rendered concrete. It is this (con)fusion of gender that Dickinson confronts and exploits in her poem of regeneration. Again, it is provoked by the use of a grammatical mark that begins the poem, the idiosyncratic, almost modernistic, use of a grammar of dashes. She begins, 'I'm ceded—I've stopped being Theirs—' and the presence of the dash is felt immediately, repeated incessantly, compulsively, as a short-hand notation throughout the poem both as a mark of a certain spacing, the space of definition ('—I've stopped being Theirs—') and of the isolation, removal and disunion ('I'm ceded—') that opens the poem. Dickinson declares again the American manifesto of individual self-determination through her declaration of independence. Moreover, this at a time when secession was a political and national reality looming on the horizons of American consciousness. Dickinson declares her *state* of individuality by refusing the claims of her forbears; like Whitman, she steps out alone.

The dash, however, renders a positive service of liberation via its negative marking. Having 'stopped being Theirs', those shadowy and threateningly possessive others, Dickinson also refuses the name they 'dropped upon [her] face/With water in the country church'. With the refusal of a name, nameless, the poet loses the vestiges of her childhood, of her infantilised existence as a 'homely' spinster: She tells us:

And They can put it with my Dolls,
My childhood, and the string of spools,
I've finished threading.

From this social and overt history of a personality, an autobiography of herself as 'every' woman, every social being,
Dickinson moves to the hidden sites of regeneration, antisocial, if
not merely non-social, irrational, individualistic and subjective.
Again, she writes:

Baptized before, without the choice,
But this time, consciously, of Grace—
Unto supremest name—
Called to my Full—The Crescent dropped—
Existence's whole Arc, filled up,
With one small Diadem.

Free of name and of socially delineated position, Dickinson
enters the 'passion' of rebirth, emptied of one self and refilled
with another. This baptism is not the descent of an orthodox
Christian spirit, nor the presence of an external 'Holy Ghost'
despite the invocation of the 'supremest name', but the gathering
of an inner spirit, self-generated which names itself. The old
Emily Dickinson of stanza one becomes the regenerate
Dickinson of stanza two; the poet of stanza one works toward
the union of poetic spirit and outward personality of stanza two.
Dickinson regains her name but no longer does it refer to social
relationships, the name rests occulted, described ('supremest
name') but not spoken outwardly. The name speaks only to the
reader inside the 'text', the body of the poem, spirit of
Dickinson; an inward writing, the name is represented by a mark
of absence, its power working *in absentia*. Thus, this marking of a
name moves the regenerate spirit of the poem but cannot be read
by outwardly turned eyes, for the name refuses externalisation.
At the moment of naming, like a taboo, the new name reveals
only its silence behind the dash that follows, 'Unto supremest
name—'.

Furthermore, this name, alien, silent and, yet, essential to
Dickinson's regenerate personality, calls into being the rest of the
poem as the future possibility of all Dickinson's personal

potential. The calling into being, 'Called to my Full' as we are told, begins after the dash that opens the space for the second half of the poem, a half that has moved from past to present and now narrates a future.

The 'small Diadem' which refers both to 'Crown' in stanza three and 'dropped…water' in stanza one, opens an image of a re-baptism and of a sovereignty gathered in. Indeed, this 'Diadem' is 'just a Crown' with the potential for personal integrity without social power: the power to free and organise oneself according to one's own laws. Thus, symbols of European kingship and queenliness act on behalf of American democratic ideals. More-over, this watery droplet, this diadem dropped on the 'crown' of Dickinson's head, contracts the macrocosm to the size of the individual microcosmic personality as the personality, imagined as the moon, goes out to correspond with the macrocosm. Dickinson tells us she is 'called' to her 'Full—the Crescent dropped—/Existence's whole Arc, filled up,/With one small Diadem'.

From such resolutions Dickinson tells of the freedom which this baptism offers, a freedom about which she crows on '[her] Father's breast' and which is encapsulated by the broken sentence and dash of potentiality at the poem's end, a dash which separates her *meditation* in language from the silence of the *action* of the regenerate, thus:

My second Rank—too small the first—
Crowned—Crowing— on my Father's breast—
A half unconscious Queen—
But this time—Adequate— Erect—
With Will to choose, or to reject—
And I choose, just a Crown—

And, yet, this conscious freedom, won at the expense of social position, and of 'rank', which has 'liberated' Dickinson from the authoritarian clutches of a fatherly patriarchy, is inevitably narrated in more ambiguous and ambivalent sexual terms that I have, as yet, delineated. The narrative is begun by, and disrupted by, a duality running through Dickinson's sexual choices. Her decisions about gender remain future potentials of a poem which deals with the sexuality of the psyche. Hence, we must return to the opening stanza to understand the necessities placed upon the poem by a women 'liberating' herself in masculine terms.

The poem begins 'I'm ceded'. As if by self-fecundation ('seeded') Dickinson separates herself from her old personality giving birth rather than being born. The spirit descends upon her, as upon Mary, but this time the action is self-generated, a casting of one's seed to rework biological possibility. Having conceived herself, the poet is 'called' to the 'Full', and reborn through the pneumatic logos (as seed). By stanza three Dickinson's second Rank has replaced a rank 'too small'. She is, through a transexualising of her father's chest, able to end by 'crowing' on 'her father's breast', resting her life and recuperating her femininity on the parodic breasts of a father obviously unable now to nurture his child, a child who has no use for her father's seed.

Moreover, this self-fertilisation is possible only by awakening the masculine sexual urge of her inner mind, which itself articulates the language of sexuality. Just as before, Dickinson 'seeds' herself, conceives herself and gives birth to herself. But, by this time, she is 'Erect'.

Indeed, we can take this a step further. By the last stanza Dickinson is ready to choose her sexuality. Yet, she does *not* choose and thus the poem stands upon the brink of a revelatory fulfilment which is encapsulated in the poem but does not potentiate itself within the poem. Here, then, the whole of existence contracts to her 'small Diadem' (that 'hairy diadem' of Donne's *Elegy Nineteen*) which focusses on the area of giving forth while not yet aware of a differentiation between sexual organs. 'A half unconscious Queen', Dickinson is neither king nor queen nor has she decided upon the potential sexuality of a 'queane'. Consequently, the decision of which 'Will to choose' (as in Shakespeare) is left as an unanswered question, poised on the possibility of a rejection of either sexual role as a singular and totalising choice. Dickinson's 'erect[ness]' is that of one whose 'adequacy' allows her *the time* to choose her new sexual role (a sexual role which directs biology but is, of course, initially freed within fantasy).

Dickinson brings sexuality into the poem through the act of 'naming', she drops their name for her in order to claim, through the 'supremest name', her *own* new name, which waits for its

10

mark of gender. The language of naming and of sexuality allows Dickinson to 'place' others and isolate them through hyphenation; it also gives her the space for the taking on of a new gender role. She is 'conscious' of her choice to regenerate but 'half unconscious' of her new possibilities, possibilities contained and held *in vitro* via an initial hyphen that 'seeds' her and allows here to 'cede' in order to accede to a new role from the old. Her seeding and ceding is negated via the hyphen as it is *expressed*. Nothingness takes the place of sexual distinction in order to make space for choice; nothingness, as a grammatical mark, unites male and female awaiting their transcendent term.

2

Sexuality, Jane Austen's Fanny and *Mansfield Park*

Mansfield Park has always proved a controversial novel. It has roused more passion and energy than any of Jane Austen's other novels, proving a thorn to the advocates of Austen's art and a weapon for those detractors who applaud the art yet wince at the conservatism. Recently, feminist critics have highlighted Austen's radicalism toward both the issue of women's emancipation and the issue of slavery and they have seen this as an indication either that *Mansfield Park* has been misread by critics over the years or that it has been obscured by a misguided interest in morality.[1] This essay is an attempt to reconsider Austen's conservatism and to see her radicalism as one that ultimately upholds that conservatism. However, within that fundamental contradiction I wish to reconsider Austen's attitude to Fanny Price, around whom the continuing controversy rages, and to delineate the peculiar role Price plays, not merely in the novel, but as a *relational notation* between Austen, the text and the reader. Indeed, although it anticipates my argument, I propose Fanny not just as a young girl in a novel but as that very element that functions as *ambiguity* in our reading and in Austen's imaginary project for her novel. For Fanny indicates a *prior* moment to Austen's narrative inclinations or moral requirements. Fanny represents an opening and closing of an imaginative moment into which a novel of morals was to fit.

It is a commonplace among literary critics that *Mansfield Park* is about moral education. This obvious remark accepts the *prima facie* case put by Austen herself that against the lack of 'self-knowledge, generosity and humility' (Ch. 2) of her 'adopted' family cousins Fanny with her 'pretty' face and social naïveté should represent the fundamental goodness (that very 'self-knowledge' and 'humility') that her 'betters' lacked. In this Austen accentuates nature against nurture, humility against pride and moral awareness (as empathic rightness of action) against moral laxity (shown by Austen as changeable or *wayward* personality). Fanny's moral superiority is then primarily founded in her unchangeable nature, a nature whose 'education' confirms and finally ordains her in her new-found position; this Fanny learns self-knowledge only by osmosis. She represents the correctness of a mental and moral stasis which is grounded in a type of 'trueness' to self: a 'concern for the nature of selfhood'[2].

Interestingly, this stasis is an ironic form of *activity* if it is counterposed to Lady Bertram's indolence which is the epitome of a social role so caricatured as to make plain a further moral lesson about sloth. This sloth is what prepares the ground for the waywardness of Lady Bertram's daughters for 'to the education of her daughters she paid not the smallest attention'(Ch. 2). Indolence actively promotes evil.

Lady Bertram represents (through her disinterest in her role as a mother) the *negation* of responsibility, a responsibility to self that is denied by her refusal to take any active part in the education of her daughters. Thus her indolence becomes itself wayward but immobile. Fanny, however, actively discovers her 'true' self by the very imposed passivity that her social circumstances force upon her. The fruitless moral activity of Lady Bertram's needlework is contrasted to Fanny's morally fruitful passivity as audience to the antics of the family; Fanny is watchful, alert, on guard while Lady Bertram is obviously not. Moral laxity therefore represents movement which goes nowhere—movement positively dangerous in defence of one's 'honour'.

Maria's waywardness leads not merely to 'ruin' and divorce but is punished by immurement: the adventurer finally becomes a nun closetted with Aunt Norris, for 'she must withdraw…to retirement and reproach, which could allow no second spring of hope or character' (Ch. 48). Indeed, we are told 'something must have been wanting *within* [italics mine]' (Ch. 48) which precedes the statement that though 'instructed theoretically in religion

[she] had never [been] required to bring it into daily practice' (Ch. 48). This fault is brought about by 'mismanagement', a familial corollary to Sir Thomas' necessary trip to his Antiguan slave holdings to put more careful management into practice there.

Religion, therefore, represented as 'social ethics' reveals true character. Social management brings out *the true* and *the correct* and thus religion becomes a practical social guide to self-knowledge. This self-knowledge is seen, nevertheless, to be intrinsic to *self* and yet at the same time a product of *social* management. Religious activity in the social sphere allows the individual to find herself in her own private sphere (but the private is nowhere anything else other than social, that is, *public*). Paradoxically, however, the social activity of the Bertrams and their friends courts moral opprobrium while to 'act' correctly is not to act at all.

This clearly brings us to the scene of the theatrical rehearsals. Again, inactivity is stressed—they are precisely rehearsals. It is the return of Sir Thomas' 'good government' (Ch. 21) that keeps them just that. As before with the scene in the 'wilderness' and, as later, in the return of Fanny to her 'real' home in Portsmouth, chaos threatens the order of Mansfield. Mansfield's social order, commercially based on slavery (which itself is threatened) awaits its moral order (represented by the finally 'reconstellated' family) to secure its position.

The immorality of the theatricals represents not merely a threat to order from sexual foreplay and innuendo but more im-portantly the threat to order posed by acting itself, clearly referred to as an 'infection' brought by Mr Yates. Sexuality and 'infection' (Ch. 19) unite in the concept of acting. Against this acting the social constraints and restraints of accepting a social role and acting it out are exposed. We are told that for Fanny 'it would be horrible to act' (Ch. 16) and so the notion of social role as natural role is reinforced. Fanny's social role, unhampered by the 'acting' that comes from education allows her to remain 'naturally' on the side of an order which awaits the return of the patriarch Sir Thomas.

Here, then, for Austen one type of acting is immorally active (Rushworth looks forward to returning home and 'doing nothing') and dangerously explosive (Ch. 19). The *real* nature of the actors is exposed through their parts and thus Austen undermines the very notion of artifice. Ironically, the acted *becomes* the real and indivisible from it: theatre becomes life and life theatre through 'infection' (as in Artaud's 'Theatre and the Plague').

Conversely, for Austen, Fanny's nature (*unimproved* and romantic—we note all those improving gardeners) accords with a hidden moral reality which has been *exposed* to view throughout the novel and yet is only seen for what it is at the end. Fanny plays the 'invisible woman', to be looked 'through' until the novel's end. Hence, Fanny never deals in the hidden in her moral action (although she is always overlooked) whereas the others expose their social morality as artificial precisely when they act. As Edmund says to her, 'you seem[ed] almost as fearful of notice...as other women of neglect' (Ch. 38). Hence, the hidden Fanny, so hidden that 'it is so dark you do not see her' (Ch. 38) is really the exposed. Fanny's single and unified state of moral awareness is placed against the split nature of the morality of her peers.

Up to this point the nature versus nurture debate has been guided along a careful line of demarcation: acting is seen ironically as being both the perverse outcome of immorality and when 'acting true to nature' (as with Fanny) totally laudable. Movement and social mobility are also seen as both ironically morally lapsed and (as with Fanny whose inner moral movement leads to social mobility) utterly laudable. Social and personal movement are dichotomised as belonging to the outward sphere and (as again with Fanny) the far better inner sphere which unite only at the end with social action (marriage). Art itself is posed as both morally corrupting and perfectly synonymous with moral responsibility.

In each case the problem is centred on Austen's relation to her 'heroine' Fanny whose nature is in accord with a social propriety exposed only at the harmonious end of the novel. Fanny, while 'hidden', acts as the unifying core of the narrative and when 'exposed' she acts as the moral/personal goal of the narrative. While the novel's plot is based on characters being 'exposed' to us through Fanny, Fanny herself is denied a character until all the others are dismissed at the novel's end. Thus Fanny appears peculiarly opaque. This opaqueness leads to the clarity of Fanny's marriage which represents the comic return to social stability, the totalising effect of Mansfield's social stasis (her sister replaces her in her old position) and by her absorption with the expelling of the immoral 'others'. A suitable end to the Cinderella theme in which class mobility is ironically possible only if that mobility dignifies, justifies and constitutes the immobility (represented by notions of order and harmony) of the ruling class. The fickle changeability of the 'modern' psyche socially represented in contemporary improvements to gardens and houses is sharply contrasted to the unchangeable virtues of Fanny (Mr Rushworth's 'improvements' (Ch. 9) include leaving off daily prayers). When Fanny wishes to find a mechanism to recall memory she says to Miss Crawford:

> Every time I come into this shrubbery I am more struck with its growth and beauty. Three years ago, this was nothing but a rough hedgerow along the upper side of the field, never thought of as any thing, or capable of becoming any thing; and now it is converted into a walk, and it would be difficult to say whether most valuable as a convenience or an ornament; and perhaps in another three years we may be forgetting—almost forgetting what it was before...If any one faculty of our nature may be called *more* wonderful than the rest, I do think it is memory. There seems something more speakingly incomprehensible in the powers, the failures, the inequalities of memory, than in any other of our intelligences. The memory is sometimes so retentive, so serviceable, so obedient—at others, so bewildered and so weak—and at others again, so tyrannic, so beyond control'.—We are to be sure a miracle every way—but our powers of recollecting and of forgetting, do seem peculiarly past finding out. (Ch. 22)

Fanny states of nature what Fanny becomes. Fanny functions as Mansfield's memory; a reconstitution of the old against the encroachments of the new. Hence, the past becomes the 'future' of Mansfield.

Fanny's 'natural' nature (shown as really 'noble') puts the approving seal on the natural right of Mansfield to dominate Northamptonshire society. Fanny finds her rightful home and rightful father as nobility of morals complements and fuses with social 'nobility'. Each constellation of ideas and themes focusses on the ever-present, ever-invisible Fanny, exposed and yet hidden, ever justifying a certain status quo from the 'charity' she receives and the charitable (i.e. humble) nature she adopts. Nevertheless, she represents a constant threat to that status quo (as she is exposed to the reader) by being too closely related to Portsmouth and to the 'viewpoint' of the author, Jane Austen.

How the order at Mansfield is reconstituted, and the relationship Fanny has to the moral purpose of Austen's art, are the questions to which I shall now turn in order to reconsider some of the possible interpretations of Fanny's status as a prerequisite of Austen's artistic project and as a character embodying that project in the novel.

Austen's narrative begins many years before Fanny's arrival at Mansfield. Of the three Ward sisters one marries perversely (a theme repeated with her niece) one marries 'properly' and another, although married, acts as if she is a spinster with the caricatured attributes of a spinster's mentality. A social, familial and sexual set of differences are set in motion. Lady Bertram and her family are placed between Fanny's mother Frances, her lower-class setting, obscenely gross family and inability to avoid yet another pregnancy and Aunt Norris the crabbed and penny-pinching 'frigid' curate's wife. While Lady Bertram is seen as a none too perfect mother her abstinence after four children is in marked contrast to Frances' 'ninth lying in' (Ch. 1) and Mrs Norris' childless state.

It is, however, Frances' lower-class status as well as that of Mrs Norris that condemns them to either a 'superfluity of children' (Ch. 1) or none at all: income dictates family size in inverse proportion to wealth as the opening paragraph of the novel clearly shows.

The perverse marriage of Frances to a 'lieutenant of Marines, without education, fortune, or connections' (Ch. 1) condemns her to continual sexual activity (a result of her *predisposition* before marriage to perversity). 'Intercourse' (Austen's term) between sisters slips into intercourse between drunken husband and sluttish wife (Ch. 1). While Frances' sister Mrs Norris is essential to the plot of *Mansfield Park* she represents a social superfluity in her role as 'spinster' (married or otherwise) just as Frances represents an excess with her 'superfluity of children'

(Ch. 1). Both, either through frigidity or overt sexual activity, represent an *excess* in the novel that needs to be dismissed for Mansfield to survive. Frances is 'lost' after her daughter's visit to Portsmouth as Mrs Norris is sent into exile with the daughter that repeats Frances' crime of perversity of will at the end. In the figure of Julia (Frances' surrogate) Frances and Mrs Norris are forced out of the sanctuary of Mansfield as the denotations of its limit. Though they represent a threat in the beginning they are neutralised as this limit at the end. Fanny, Frances' daughter, (herself called 'Fanny') atones for her mother's perversity by finding the real nature of Fannys at Mansfield and thus neutralises her mother's perversity of will. Fanny, the product of an excess that is horribly obvious (she is a reminder of her mother's inability to avoid sexual activity), is rendered invisible. From a Portsmouth family in which no one (*not even servants*) know their place, she finds her place at Mansfield.

It is thus the very notion of the superfluous, the 'thing' unnecessary to the order, that ends as a principle of unity and organisation and the essential ingredient of that order. The threat of excess (represented by the lower orders — Fanny's family, the representatives of chaos through excess of drink, of children) is absorbed into the social hierarchy until it finally acts as the justification of that hierarchy and its central unifying principle. The threat is thus recuperated by that order as its most consistent defence: Fanny finds her real home only when she finds the nobility of her morals (out of place in Portsmouth). Thence, the bigger Fanny's family the more of an orphan (in all senses) she becomes. On every level she reconstitutes her own family (chooses and passively remodels them *through us* as readers) in a version of wish-fulfilment and family romance, allowing Sir Thomas to 'adopt' 'the daughter he wanted' (Ch. 48).

Fanny's passivity is rewarded with marriage to her first cousin/'brother' Edmund and this is prefigured by her *ordination* at the behest of Edmund in the scene with the necklaces. Here, Fanny symbolically takes on the values not only of Edmund and William but also of Maria Crawford. Thus, Maria's eroticism is joined to Edmund and William's cross and chain. Symbolically two 'brothers' exchange the erotic sister and the 'sister' becomes the symbolic embodiment of an eroticised Christian subjugation (the necklace: chain: slavery: Antigua):

She had, to oblige Edmund, resolved to wear it—but it was too large for the purpose. His therefore must be worn; and having, with delightful feelings, joined the chain and the cross, those memorials of the two most beloved of her heart, those dearest tokens so formed for each other by every thing real and imaginary—and put them round her neck, and seen and felt how full of William and Edmund they were, she was able, without an effort, to resolve on wearing Miss Crawford's necklace too. She acknowledged it to be right. Miss Crawford had a claim. (Ch. 27)

Law, which is considered as an option for Edmund by Maria and which Edmund finds unacceptable, (but which is nevertheless upheld by him) and religion unite with moral and social correctness and 'constrict' the eroticism of Fanny's throat. Through this 'ordination' Fanny takes on Maria's eroticism (female allure) only to have it constrained within her brothers' religiosity and law. When Fanny quotes Dr Johnson's maxim 'as to matrimony and celibacy' (Ch. 39) Austen makes it quite clear, that although Fanny is thinking of her two homes, she does so exclusively in terms of marriage (sexual activity, like her mother) and celibacy (chastity or moral virginity). Fanny marries to *remain* chaste and therefore her mother's perversity is exorcised. Edmund's sexual anaesthesia obviously plays a part here as he thinks of Fanny only as his 'sister' (Ch. 46). Mansfield represents celibacy and its attendant 'pain' (Ch. 46) which is conspicuously displayed by Fanny's life as a 'nun' in her fireless cell in the attic (Ch. 32). Henry Crawford's reading from Shakespeare's *Henry the Eighth* (Ch. 34) reminds us that a girl can always lose her head but Fanny's marriage, both rational and religious, allows her to keep her 'head' despite matrimony. Chastity becomes a moral as well as physical attribute.

Austen's authorial and authoritative declaration of 'my Fanny' (Ch. 48) enforces the morality of Fanny's position (a reverse *missionary position*: see the remarks on Edmund and 'missionary' (Ch. 47) work at the novel's close) in which the naïve natural child from Portsmouth civilises Mansfield society and gets her man. A man, nevertheless, whose sexual anaesthesia reinforces chastity as a marital goal (the author remained unmarried) and as a narrational goal. Through the initial importance of Fanny, 'survivor' of the tale, and through her belonging to the authorial possessive, Austen's declaration reinforces an ownership which upholds Fanny's position as authority and yet seems to deny that position as she becomes an object for authorial possession. Fanny lives as Austen's possession and as *our* possession as Austen steps out of silence to declare her interest. In so doing Fanny gets out of control (Austen is seen to make a mistake—a 'wrong' note is sounded), the reader is alerted and Austen is robbed. Austen steps back to admire her possession and in so doing becomes a reader trapped by the 'glamour' of her text. Fanny's escape leaves her in suspension, freed from Austen, lost by the possessive 'my' to her readers.

Fanny's suspension is ironically brought about only after she becomes a person *in her own right*.

Yet she only becomes such a person with regard to a lending library and 'she becomes a subscriber—annoyed at being anything in *propria persona*, annoyed at her own doings in every way' (Ch. 40). However, through such action she is literally consigned to a bookshelf—a person (having attained self-hood and self-possession) only in connection with the *circulation* of books finally and ironically *lent* to her. After this she is capable (the only possibility now?) of acting on her own responsibility (relinquishing responsibility?) by marrying (becoming the wife *of*) Edmund.

By this process Fanny leaves the reader and the text in suspense. She connects without signifying until she signifies within a text but only in relation to texts. Her life is suspended in a library but is no longer invisible; Fanny's suspension 'connects' the various areas in the book. She holds life (the false morality and *activity* of the sisters and the Crawfords) and death (the stasis of her marriage to Edmund and its morality) within her bounds. She connects Austen to her readers and herself becomes a reader (of the library books). Disconnect a Fanny (cut a Fanny up) and she remains a Fanny complete. Austen's *cogito* 'represented' by Fanny in Austen's possessive exclamation becomes *cogito interruptus*: a *cogito* in suspension between life and death.

Fanny acts as a fantastic fay held within and acting upon a web of textual fate: a conjunction that becomes a predicate (she is the 'being' of Mansfield). Fanny, so often excluded, is included only at a great risk—all sexual deviation is expelled. Female lust

(Maria and Julia) is controlled or expunged and Fanny remains Fanny intacta. Fanny is broken and dissected by the others at Mansfield and Portsmouth. For both she signifies excess—waste and inappropriate existence suspended between two life-styles which both reject her (Fanny is merely the brunt of a dirty joke by her father). When she is finally 'placed' we (the history of critical readers) 'reject' her and suspend her between Austen (her 'my Fanny' literally gets in the way) and our acceptance—the 'female' here signifies only when broken or ignored.

The familial/marital bonds reinforce this: Fanny is suspended between legitimacy and incestuousness. (Is not Edmund Shakespeare's Bastard?). Not only have we seen the symbolic exchange of Fanny (which only leaves her affection greater for *both* brothers) by Edmund and William but Sir Thomas finds a *daughter* to give to his *son*. Austen's 'my Fanny' is suspended between that exclamation and the claim of Edmund who also declares 'my Fanny—my only sister' (Ch. 46). Fanny is sister/wife to Edmund and 'sister'/daughter to Austen (a point to which we shall return). Moreover, Fanny is well aware (while in another 'displaced' connection) of the incestuous possibilities of the family connections, for she announces after learning of Mrs Maria Rushworth's absconding with Henry Crawford:

> Fanny seemed to herself never to have been shocked before. There was no possibility of rest. The evening passed, without a pause of misery, the night was totally sleepless. She passed only from feelings of sickness to shudderings of horror; and from hot fits of fever to cold. The event was so shocking, that there were moments even when her heart revolted from it as impossible—when she thought it could not be. A woman married only six months ago, a man professing himself devoted, even *engaged*, to another—that other her near relation—the whole family, both families connected as they were by tie upon tie, all friends, all intimate together! — it was too horrible a confusion of guilt, too gross a complication of evil, for human nature, not in a state of utter barbarism, to be capable of!—yet her judgement told her it was so. (Ch. 46)

Fanny is only aware of passion with 'a near relation', of the

21

complications around the intimacy of the two 'families' and of a 'too horrible confusion of guilt'. Incest unites and destroys the bonds of unity. It acts as the unspoken and contradictory principle of unity for the familial ties of the novel. As a principle of unity it descends upon us through its benign aspect with Fanny's marriage and its diabolical aspect in adultery. Fanny articulates (actually articulates only the resultant horror) both sides and thus she suspends the taboo in and through her own presence for she is the one who meditates upon the unmentionable *and* acts out its ritual in 'morganatic' marriage. Incest is both a superfluous threat and an essential bonding ingredient of the novel's plot.

But this familial/textual bond goes further. Fanny is superfluous and essential. Her very superfluousness makes her ironically essential. Always extraneous to the two families and to the acting of the action (to the narrative) she nevertheless acts as a principle of unity (not *the* principle for she acts only as the agent of unification for Mansfield).

Austen exudes Fanny as a superfluity of imagination. She gives artistic birth to Fanny, but she reclaims her too. Fanny is *not* just another character in the text. She is the *pretext* and the *context* for the action of the others in their relationship with the reader. Ordination remains the critical theme—the calling of the elect and the being chosen. Fanny is the doubly chosen by Edmund and by Austen.

Fanny is superfluous and essential in another sense. She is an *agent* and a *conjunction* in the text which unites the oppositional worlds of Portsmouth and Mansfield. She acts only to deny herself until Maria and Julia, the ugly sisters in this retelling of *Cinderella*, are themselves expelled. But what is the significance of the Cinderella theme to Fanny's function in and as a precondition of the text?

My concluding speculations are prefaced by a consideration of the Cinderella myth in *Mansfield Park*. In these remarks I follow the highly interesting application of Freud's discussion of 'The Theme of the Three Caskets' by Avrom Fleishman in his book *A Reading of Mansfield Park*. Fleishman notes that Freud's analysis covered *King Lear*, a play that Austen went to see while writing her novel in which she included a Tom, an Edmund, a foolish father, two bad sisters and one good one. As with Cordelia so Fanny, 'makes herself unrecognizable' and remains 'dumb' for most of the novel.[3]

Quoting Freud, Fleishman points out:

> 'We may perhaps be allowed to equate concealment and dumbness. [Freud] goes on to make the further equation of dumbness and death: the chosen women are usually pale, ethereal creatures whose love has something bloodless, otherworldly, and renunciatory about it. If we accept this thesis, we may be prepared to follow Freud in his most agile imaginative leap: 'But if the third of the sisters is the Goddess of Death, the sisters are known to us. They are the Fates, the Moerae, the Parcae or the Norns, the third of whom is called Atropos, the inexorable.'[4]

Anticipating the reader's objection to this idea of Cinderella as the ugliest of the sisters instead of the prettiest we are told that:

> At this point the reader impatient with psychoanalytic associationism might object that the third of the daughters, far from being the most macabre of deities, is the most desirable, most loving, even—as in Paris's choice of Aphrodite—most beautiful. Freud acknowledges and speculates on the duality of the chosen one, and finds it at the heart of the Cinderella story: it is eventually the ugliest who is fairest; in *Lear*, it is the coldest who is most loving. The choice which opens greatest possibilities of happiness is precisely the one men seem most to abhor. We are in a better position now to appreciate the irrational hostility which Fanny Price has almost universally evoked: she is at once the most attractive and the most repulsive character in the novel, and the only appropriate response to her is a deeply ambivalent one.[5]

We may summarise as follows: although Fanny is 'pretty' compared to her sisters (with their sexual and social allure) she is the ugly menial. Her honest plainness is then equated with ugliness while her morality 'kills' any life that the others may show. It is her morals, nevertheless, which give her beauty. As for

Fanny, it is she who (via her mother the first Fanny), initiates the action and acts as its moral *telos*. Her marriage with Edmund seals the fate of Mansfield Park's moral and ethical practice in the future (for, as the novel ends there, the future acts effectively as a fated end and history stops—driven back by and through Fanny). We have noted Fanny's ambivalent position through-out—passive, voyeuristic, priggish, sexually anaemic, unerotic and yet morally active, unaffected, hard done by, loving, marriageable.

In and through this ambiguity fateful Fanny becomes the agent and avatar of the death drive, for Fleishman tells us:

> In this view, the organism tends to return to its origins, finding there a lower level of activity or none at all. That is, the organism tends toward death, in which there is no painful expenditure of energy at all. The attraction to death is itself, paradoxically, a pursuit of pleasure, and conversely, as Freud concludes, 'The pleasure principle seems actually to serve the death-instincts.'[6]

Fleishman caustically adds:

> Fanny Price is the chief spokesman for life denial. Although she affirms her love for at least two persons, Edmund and her brother William, her typical response is to deny: the theatricals, the courtship of Henry, even her parents. Fanny may not be an acceptable symbol of death itself, but it is her role to deny the pleasures of life in favor of the pleasures of principle, which feel like death. Edmund turns to her only after his love for a vivacious woman is blighted, and he does so resignedly, for one who can love Fanny is ready to embrace death, too.[7]

Here is the central issue of critical ambiguity and critical 'confusion' over the 'meaning' of the novel. Fanny is the super-fluity that threatens life (as death) yet upholds it (as the unity of life). She finally becomes the superfluous as centre—a dead centre, driven by the lowering of pleasure to 'death' itself: *total stasis.*

As this 'plus—centre' (the centrality of the superfluous) she acts as pretext for the story. Fanny is the opening through which the story is presented. Her static position allows the story to be given. From Fanny, Austen's art is brought into the world. Fanny is Austen's imaginative conduit which Austen claims back as her own—at once necessarily expelled from Austen as an imaginative placenta, a placenta which Laing speculates is our original brother/sister/twin to which our initial references are made and our fantasy referrals to the 'other' are 'actually' directed. Our placenta is then our original lost origin, both 'born' and 'dead' upholding and confronting life.[8]

Fanny performs this role for Austen as author and for the reader of her novel. The 'dead' or the *lost* child (recall Sir Thomas finding a *daughter* for his son, her 'brother') is one which cannot be forgotten. She is always the good, the better, the possibility of renewal *elsewhere* on the plateau of death. Fanny is the superfluous origin—the core of the book through which and into which interpretation is expelled and absorbed.

Virginia Wolf in *A Room of One's Own* tells us that art is 'not life' and 'life conflicts with something that is not life' Art is *not-life* representing life. *Not-life* is expressed into the world by Austen as artist and it is Fanny who *is* the process (rather than a mere character) of that expression, expulsion, recovery. Fanny's dissection by the critics—her ambivalence—makes her a 'failure' and a necessity for the novel's form. Austen, I suggest, could not 'do without' the built-in failure of her main character—a character so alive to Austen that we are told by Austen that she is writing her 'biography' in the novel (Ch. 48). Fanny is chased and chaste, escaping both writer and reader.

Fanny is Austen's imaginative twin/baby/placenta. Hence imaginative incest. Austen takes her back and gives her away again. Like the first Fanny, Fanny Price *née* Ward, Fanny is the restoration of the guilty Fanny but Fanny *without* children. Childless and non-sexual against her mother's overt sexuality (whose spillage produces her *other* Fanny) her not-self daughter becomes a ghostly oppositional double. Fanny, her mother and Austen begin the narrative of inability to abstain from sexual activity. Sexuality is *overproduction* as imaginative potential. Fanny becomes a possibility, a relational space, a conjunction—an opening where creative imagination and death can unite. Fanny produces a Fanny to produce a tale and so the second Fanny reconstitutes and restores the equilibrium of all Fannys in Austen's world. The mother, nevertheless, in this world, produces yet another static niece in Susan, Fanny's sister, who is herself another spillage and another waste product of Portsmouth. Useless as a daughter Susan becomes valuable as a niece (Ch. 48). Mansfield Park lives off the waste products of Portsmouth: waste female bodies from the baby machine. The sister self-exiled produces the 'sister' exiled and finally accepted. Fanny, the mother, is reconstituted and therefore acceptable through the quest of her daughter (the *other* Fanny, the acceptable Fanny).

Austen's two Fannys equate and cancel—the daughter pays for and pays off the sins of the mother. Hence, one Fanny *opens* the tale for another to *close* the tale and the production line *and* the chain of possible readings. A Fanny opens for 'birth' and closes for 'death', Life produces *not-life* and the artist produces her art.

The reader completes his or her moral education.

3

The 'Humunculus'

Marie Bonaparte's, *The Life and Works of Edgar Allan Poe* and Poe's 'The Facts in the Case of M. Valdemar'. Psychobiography, possession of the body, manipulation of the body, parody, transference and the 'return' of the body

Psychoanalysis is 'deep' biography, a charting of the hidden motives and the most private phantasies of its subject.[1] Freud, whose case histories always have this 'deep' biographical nature, was interested in the ambivalent motives behind biographical endeavours:

> But what can these biographies achieve for us? Even the best and fullest of them could not answer the two questions which alone seem worth knowing about. It would not throw any light on the riddle of the miraculous gift that makes an artist, and it could not help us to comprehend any better the value and the effect of his works ... it is, then, the need to acquire affective relations with such men, to add them to the fathers, teachers, exemplars whom we have known or whose influence we have already experienced, in the expectation that their personalities will be just as fine and admirable as those works of art of theirs which we possess .... All the same, we may admit that there is still another motive force at work. The biographer's justification also contains a confession. It is true that the biographer does not want to depose his hero, but he does want to bring him nearer to us. That means, however, reducing the distance that separates him from us: it still tends in effect towards degradation.[2]

Thus, Freud expresses a distaste for biography even as he

condones its value by his practice.

It is these injunctions 'against' biography that preface our inquiry into Marie Bonaparte's *Life and Works of Edgar Allan Poe*. In her work we will see not only a writer attempting to provide some 'light on the riddle of the miraculous gift that makes an artist', but also one whose text (as 'confession') tries to 'depose' its hero, and by bringing him nearer to us dispossess him of his texts in a form of 'degradation'. If such 'degradation' (a word of high emotional charge) is possible, how does a biography 'justify' itself in its very 'confession' and what form does the biographical style take in its endeavour at once to degrade its subject and yet to *elevate* it by discovering the 'miraculous gift that makes an artist'? For Marie Bonaparte it was, at least partially, to 'interpret' Poe's 'genius' by *translating* it into the language of psychoanalysis.

To begin in the paradoxical world of priority revealed in Bonaparte's text, Freud stands for us as the precursor of Poe as well as the newcomer, the son coming in priority to the father, the father begotten by the son. This reversal is made explicit by Marie Bonaparte when she writes, 'that is why Poe opposes the force of Attraction, equated in *Eureka* with the death-instinct, with the force of Repulsion equated there with the life-instinct'.[3] History is turned inside out and in viewing Poe *through* Freud we see how Poe anticipates Freud and, by so doing, is only interpretable, according to Bonaparte, by using Freud's concepts. Poe is therefore prior to, and yet somehow comes 'after', Freud's ideas, 'thus the Son, in his turn, begets the Father and, in his narcissism becomes the Father in his turn'.[4] Harold Bloom has seen this as the first 'revision' of the new text attempting to find its own voice:

> Clinamen; this appears as a corrective movement...which implies that the precursor poem went accurately up to a certain point, but then should have swerved, precisely in the direction that the new poem moves... but the poem is now *held* open to the precursor, where once it *was* open, and the uncanny effect is that the new poem's achievement makes it seem to us, not as though the precursor were writing it, but as though the later poet himself had written the precursor's characteristic work.[5]

This movement is observable in Marie Bonaparte's appraisal of Poe's 'achievement' in 'understanding' the forces to which psychoanalysis would give a name. Of *Eureka*'s similar hypothesis to physics she writes, 'one might ask whether this vision of a final annihilation of Matter, which in certain ways seems to forecast one of the concepts of modern physics and, therefore, may appear possessed of high objective value to some, was not also inspired in Poe by deeply personal and subjective complexes'.[6]

However, says Bonaparte, this similarity is merely perverse. Although it would appear that *Eureka* seems an early precursor of modern physics, Bonaparte denies that relationship by assigning stereotyped images both to physics and to Poe. Physics, to use her phraseology, must contain 'high objective value', but *Eureka*, while it 'appears' to possess such objectivity, is only possessed of 'deeply personal and subjective complexes'. Thus, Poe's essay is made illegitimate on the grounds that it contains a personal, rather than universal validity. This statement from Bonaparte is necessary if she is to turn a *comparative* appraisal into one dominated by, (because always 'anchored' in), the act of an analysing discourse. Poe is rendered a fit subject for analysis because Bonaparte has not acknowledged that Poe's thesis in *Eureka* illegitimises neither subjective nor objective knowledge (man partaking of part of the godhead) and that this is precisely why, according to Poe, objectivity can accrue from the subjective complex. Indeed, because of Poe's conception of 'God', intuition (the complex) and objectivity (mathematics and logic) are interdependent.

We can, however, observe this movement (of differentiation and denial) by the analyst in a more detailed passage. Bonaparte here reverses the implications of Poe's *Eureka* in order to finalise his subjugation not merely as a text to be inserted into a discourse (that of psychoanalysis) but also as a patient, whose body, as 'text', needs to be 'cured'.

The passages to which Bonaparte refers are those in which Poe tries to account for the invisible flux of the spiritual universe—a process which will lead him eventually to consider the aether in a purely metaphysical way—that is, as a medium for speculation and produced by speculation. It is then in the first instance Bonaparte *herself* who regards these passages 'as specially significant' because they have disturbed Bonaparte as a repetition *before the fact* of Freud's 'discovery' of the libidinal flux. 'Indeed', says Bonaparte, 'strange as at first sight it appears to our mind Poe's principle of 'Repulsion corresponds ... with what we call libido'.[7] 'To our mind': in other words Poe's essay has been projected on to by Bonaparte quite simply because Poe could not have known about libido. It is Bonaparte herself ('our mind') who finds the libido here. No wonder she considers it 'strange' to do so. In a literal sense then Bonaparte must 'repulse' this idea in Poe as a strange imitation of a psychoanalytic concept.

To accomplish this corrective swerve, which will place the order of priority in reverse, Bonaparte uses the tactics of the rhetorical question in order to isolate Poe from the reader, whose complicity must be with the analyst. She asks, 'is not libido terrible and strange?' as she continues to treat libido as a fact to which Poe can reply only with the vague metaphors that Bonaparte feels she has discerned *behind* Poe's words, 'is it not light, heat, magnetism and electricity?'.[8]

This distancing allows the analyst to speak both as the authoritative voice of the body of analytic research and also as the reader's guide. '*And do we* [italics mine] not know what is generally symbolized by electricity, magnetism?'[9] Indeed we do, says Bonaparte, for they are the invisible influences which assail the paranoiac 'those "effluvia" whose real significance the paranoiac so well indicates when he maintains that his persecutors employ them to bombard and torment him'.[10] It is through these influences that Bonaparte is able not only to analyse Poe's texts but also more importantly to create a certain relationship between Poe's texts and her own dominating discourse.

Thus, Poe becomes the 'classic' case for psychoanalytic treatment. His very action in *Eureka* legitimises the term libido as a psychoanalytic tool, because Poe both *demonstrates* its power, and 'understands' how it works while never naming it. 'These influences', says Bonaparte, 'correspond to real sex excitations in the subject and if, as some physiologists think, nervous charges are more or less electrical, paranoiacs, in their way, may not be altogether wrong'. 'Paranoiacs in their way, may not be altogether wrong': the paranoiac displays through psychoanalysis what psychoanalysis says belongs to its field of study proper. The paranoiac legitimises the terminology of psychoanalysis which will be gathered back from the paranoiac as an 'objective' symptom.

Ironically, the paranoiac (here, of course, Edgar Allan Poe) generates the very terminology that will authorise the analysis to so name him.

The final swerve neutralises Poe's argument and, having shown it to be merely an aberration of the author Poe's temperament, allows for the text of *Eureka* (as a giant symptom) to be dispensed with and Poe as a 'biological' individual to be dealt with. 'May we not', asks Bonaparte, 'here, in this obscure passage, see an echo of the pattern of Poe's own sex life?'[11] Hence, Bonaparte begins with a comparison on which Poe and Freud are equal, reverses Poe's position, so that Freud's libido comes first, and then uses that very term to conjecture about Poe as a subject of analysis. This reversal has led to a 'suppression' of the Poe text.

Poe, as the neurotic (the 'paranoiac' as Bonaparte exaggeratedly calls him) is now available to the form of psycho-biography Bonaparte intends to write. Poe, the subject of psycho-biography, finds his texts used as screens upon which and through which the flickerings of his symptoms become visible. His texts, then, become 'pages we need not regard'.[12] However, Poe's texts and Poe's biography are brought together by Bonaparte in such a way that the constitution of the historical individual Poe is seen to oscillate with its 'double': the character of Poe in his work, seen through a textual analysis that invokes biography and aesthetic criticism, reformulating them in the language of psychoanalysis. The constitution of Poe as a subject for literary and biographical speculation becomes intimately part of the narrative of analysis that Bonaparte weaves, a narrative woven of strands of Poe's texts and 'known' biographical details, now given a structure through psychoanalysis. The relationship of Marie Bonaparte to Freud (through his concepts) and Poe (through his work) is then brought into focus.

We might ask as we watch the text unfold who is being analysed, who is being constituted? The reply of the analysed and the authority of (Freud) the master, render the limits of the text, both as a psychoanalytic study and as a moment of biographical and literary criticism, through a text that denies the possibility of literature even as it analyses it. This is simply because for Bonaparte, the texts envelop the individual as symptoms envelop a disease.

By the use of 'gradations' Bonaparte's analysis performs a

gradational-classificatory function, essentially static rather than progressive. Hence, 'a Maupassant or Zola' appear at one end of literature's spectrum with 'works written almost impersonally' (we get no mention of the horror of Maupassant's 'The Horla').[13] These writers are 'realists', the nineteenth-century 'spectator merely recording the panorama, and that they are accorded a certain priority only benefits their own work's similarity to scientific writing'.[14] Opposed to them are 'works that are wholly subjective'.[15] In this category comes Poe whose work is marked by 'more or less masked' complexes.[16] As Poe's texts are less mediated ('more or less masked') they are more available for the analytic excavations that reveal their origination in the complexes of their author. Authorial and yet unconscious intentionality, the issue around which Bonaparte's work revolves becomes, in a re-reading of Bonaparte, less interesting than the 'fictional' tech-niques which she employs to produce such a reading. Because Bonaparte's text is applied (via texts in which Freud generates her concepts) to other texts, precisely a biographical textual effect is produced, and a character called 'Poe' emerges.

Each tale by Poe is a symptomatic clue to the unravelling of a 'diseased' mind which alternates between drug addiction, thana-tophilia, impotence, displaced libidinal attachments and repressed homosexuality. Each text is rendered neutral in Bonaparte's quest to reconstruct the phantom of their author and belatedly understand his neuroses. Bonaparte looks for the principles of which the tales are the demonstrations and thus 'de-composition' of the tales becomes 'composition' of the individual veiled behind them.

André Green, his words now ironically turned against the analyst, points out that:

> this enables us to map out in such productions [the texts under analysis] the narcissistic "double" of their creator, which is neither his image, nor his own personality, but a projected construction, a configuration formed in place of the narcissistic idealization of the recipient of the work.[17]

Bonaparte now becomes, not the simple explicator of the 'medium' Poe's words, but indeed the transposer and translator of those words, brought to speak through the analyst. Thus,

Bonaparte constructs Poe as the ideal 'persona' and at the same moment constructs her own textual persona as the analyst; Bonaparte's text provides the space for this particular configuration. As a meshing of texts, Bonaparte and Poe reconstruct each other through the ever-present mediation of Freud.

Poe the neurotic has been situated by Bonaparte as the perfect patient, the 'model' patient whose body (as biological, historical, body of texts, or persona) passively awaits its inscription by the psychoanalyst. 'But the sex instinct cannot, with impunity, be so drastically repressed; it therefore revenged itself on Poe', Bonaparte's analysis continues,

> it determined his conspicuous maladjustment to reality and threw him back on drugs, which were so many flights from reality, and on the regressive gratifications of an imperfectly developed libido. Only one door, in fact, was left to him to reach full expression; namely, that of creative writing, though this was to be flung wide. It undermined him, psychically, as much as his unfortunate heredity undermined him physically and these two influences, closely twined, acted upon him sometimes as cause and, sometimes, as effect.[18]

We are reminded of Roderick Usher, his heredity and his interest in poetry. Thus, in this reduced form the 'body exists as a symptom of mental demands'.[19] Bonaparte continues, of one of Poe's poems, *Ulalame*, that, 'no doubt in that poem Poe confesses in symbolic and astral terms why he must always fail to achieve true union with women'.[20] Hence, as Anthony Wilden points out, 'the body (text) becomes a collection of bodily (textual) images; and the images of the mind ('author', textual scriptor) exhibiting all the organs of the body becomes the only way to approach ... reality'.[21]

In treating Poe's works as a 'body' and then conflating that body with the body of Poe himself, Bonaparte is able to achieve a number of things: the first of which is to make of Poe a creative author whose unconscious motivations (the 'keys' to his style) are *only available* through psychoanalysis. 'Nevertheless', Bonaparte says, 'displacement served to keep Poe ignorant, as for almost a century his readers, that these ailing sylphs were but forms of Elizabeth Arnold ... these ... will betray, to those with eyes to see the deeper and original underlying representations'.[22] Bonaparte continues, 'whoever would have found his way through all this but for the keys, the laws, revealed by Freud in his *Interpretation of Dreams*?'.[23]

The very 'displacement' that Bonaparte calls 'simple' is Poe's supposed transposing of 'real' individuals into his stories as characters. For Bonaparte the equation is simply reversible: character = real person = *motive for transposition*. The nature of the transposition is, for Bonaparte, not a literary/technical problem but a psychological/motival one, in which, as in analysis of clients, a solution is biographically available in the patient's past. 'Poe's women, with their "supernatural aura" were ... condensations of many of the women he loved: Berenice, Madeline and Eleonora, especially, reveal characteristics of Virginia his small cousin, as much as of his mother Elizabeth. The Aphrodite ... condenses Mrs. Stanard, Elmira, Frances Allan and Elizabeth Arnold'.[24]

Having made Poe into a unique case, (the creative writer) Bonaparte can now turn his 'body' into a perfect example of a general 'rule'. Furthermore, as a writer Bonaparte can now dispossess Poe of his texts, empty them out and 'refill' them with a meaning they are now required to possess. Harold Bloom has written of this event, in which the new writer (mediated through a third character as muse) empties out the appropriated text, and in which:

> an intermediary being, neither divine nor human, enters into the adept to aid him. The later poet opens himself to what he believes to be a power in the parent-poem that does not belong to the parent proper, but to a range of being just beyond that precursor. He does this, in his poem, by so stationing its relation to the parent-poem as to generalize away the uniqueness of the earlier work.[25]

Freud, as Bonaparte's *muse*, allows Bonaparte to differentiate and distance her analysis, so that Poe would be available only in the psychoanalytic terms that Bonaparte decides to apply. The similarity between Bonaparte's analysis of Poe and Freud's textual analysis of Judge Schreber's 'autobiography' is one that provides an interesting and curious conclusion to this method of 'emptying' and 'refilling' texts. Freud writes:

> He lived for a long time without a stomach, without intestines, almost without lungs, with a torn oesophagus, without a bladder, and with shattered ribs he used some-times to swallow part of his own larynx with his food. But divine miracles ('rays') always restored what had been destroyed, and therefore as long as he remains a man he is al-together immortal ... his 'femaleness' has become pro-minent instead.[26]

Initially, 'empty', Poe is restored through the 'divine rays' of the 'female' analyst, whose persona now comes to inhabit his texts until 'his "femaleness"' [had] become prominent instead. This is what, as Bonaparte notices 'permits the author to re-embody [herself?] himself in each of the characters observed' not the mere splitting of the author in his characters.[27]

Poe is formulated as a dichotomy of mind (subject/author) and body (object/text), so that the text directing the author, the body speaking the mind, becomes the dominant image. Bonaparte writes:

> But those we have cited [similar ideas to *Eureka*] will suffice to show that the human mind, wherever and whenever it thinks and feels, like other organs of the body tends to secrete a similar product.
>
> Now every man-invented cosmogony has had, as its base, the human mind. Considered cursorily, the universe could not have existed, no more than ourselves, time out of mind. Our analogical way of thinking makes us demand a beginning to all things and that they be created by a Father, in the same way that our own drew us from the Void. This exalted Father, whatever his name, according to epoch or latitude, is the Creator, God.
>
> The analogy between the creative act of a metaphysical deity and the generative act of the physical father, at times seems very accurate. Poe's Particle Proper, the initial organism which he expressly states is indivisible (uni-cellular), even seems to suggest the spermatozoon.

The return of all things to God, who receives back into himself all his own created beings—this yearning to return to God experienced, in Poe's system as in that of Plotinus, by everything that exists—to us seems a sort of expression, in metaphysical terms, of the son's great yearning for the Father to whom he has remained libidinally fixated.[28]

The creation myth that Bonaparte finds underlying Poe's cosmogony is based, she says, on the 'human mind' but only when it 'thinks ... like other organs of the body'. Hence, although the mind is the dominant image for the universe the mind is based on the functions of bodily organs. Indeed, the creative process of the universe is based upon the bodily function of sexual procreation, 'the creative act of a metaphysical deity and the generative act of the physical father'. Hence, if the process of bodily reproduction (or its inhibitions) can be traced in Poe, then the metaphysical aspect of creativity (the genesis of his tales) can also be explained. The universe becomes the fecunded symbol in which the father, having created the son, finds the son attempting, by re-fecunding the universe, to return to the unity denied by his projection into it. Thus, Bonaparte makes the universe a textual symbol for the creative act of the author, and a site for the projection of his mental demands. Bonaparte's sexual metaphor re-mythologises Poe's cosmogony in an explanation that returns the macrocosm to biological data.

Anthony Wilden in *System and Structure* writes of this metaphor that the 'body as an object opens out to a dissection and an analysis and thus can be constituted as a structure'.[29] Moreover, Wolfgang Iser points out that, 'a structure allows for easy access and retrieval of information'. Opened out the body allows itself to yield meaning. Yet it is exactly in the act of 'ascertaining the structure of a literary text' through 'the inventory of its structural features' that the analysis finds itself questioned.[30]

The paradox that this refusal creates actually allows for the appropriation of the mind more fully than hitherto possible. The text helps to 'repress' rather than liberate. Its subject (in this case the author) now becomes a suitable object for analysis. Symptomatised (textualised) by Bonaparte, Poe becomes a textual figure, a character in Bonaparte's essay with no greater status than the

characters in Poe's tales, from which Bonaparte draws conclusions about Poe himself.

By becoming a character within Bonaparte's narration with no
greater status textually than all the other characters both 'real'
and imaginary that she comments upon, Poe becomes the vehicle
and object of his own elucidation. He personifies the equation
through which he is universalised into a suitable subject for and
example of applied psychoanalysis. The 'silent' drama of Poe's
neuroses is repeated by Bonaparte not as fiction but as a form of
algebra. Thus, Bonaparte tells us of Poe's 'The Gold-Bug', 'as a
result of factors specific to Poe's childhood and early life, the
ancient and universal equation faeces=gold=child=penis declares
itself, in this model tale, in the greatly condensed and sole theme
of treasure'.[31]

On becoming the static models for psychoanalysis' dynamic
formula, Poe's tales as literature can be abandoned, so giving an
order (through their replacement by the formula) to Poe's
persona.

Here in algebra (the Freudian equation) the patient is opened
to receive his inscription within the coded formulae, the mytho-
logised order of psychoanalysis. Hence:

> to the reader, our analyses may at times have seemed over-
> much to stress these symbolic devices which, mono-
> tonously, bring everything in the universe back to the
> human prototypes—father, mother, child, our members
> and organs and, in particular the genitals. The fault,
> however is not ours,

says Bonaparte.[32]

At this point Bonaparte addresses her reader, one whom she
imagines both a sceptic and a little bored. 'To the reader', she
says, 'our analyses may at times have seemed overmuch to stress
these symbolic devices which monotonously, bring everything ...
back to the human prototypes'. This 'monotonously', recurring
pattern Bonaparte points out is the essential structural element
not only of literature but of life. It structures Poe's tales but it
also *replaces* them and in so doing 'explains' them. The
monotony of the equation faeces=penis finally gives a structural
order to the analysis and allows the scientist ('our analyses ...

bring everything ... back to the human'), having apologised ('the fault ... is not ours'), to gain the confidence of the reader through the 'trustworthiness' of the *repetition* of the formula itself.

One technique whereby Bonaparte is able to perform this emptying of Poe's texts and reversal of authority is paraphrase, but a paraphrase in which the technique of 'parody' (ironic imitation) is dominant. As Poe often consciously wrote parodies it is interesting and will presently be important to turn to his technique.

Therefore, it is to parody that we now turn. Poe often exploited satire at the expense of his more serious work. The *Southern Literary Messenger* of 1835 reviewing Poe called his work 'humourous, delicate satires'.[33] Before looking at Poe's work as parody it may be useful to ask in this context: what is the function of parody? Parody opens a space through the 'serious' work by finding the 'slips' that give away the processes of textual production in that work. It then reproduces the stylistic techniques of the work. These the parodic work exaggerates and thus parody becomes a specially adapted way of presenting the grotesque. By its exaggeration of technique parody highlights and questions the processes of writing.[34]

One can see this movement, the birth of the serious work alongside its double, the parodic counterpart, if we compare Poe's 'Ligeia'—a tale he thought to be his best, and one which leaves the reader at the point of revelation—with his 'The Man that was Used Up', an absurd tale of comic anticipation and grotesque denouément. If we compare their openings we can see that in 'The Man that was Used Up', Poe deliberately sets out to reproduce a 'Ligeia-like' tale but as comic by using the very elements that 'Ligeia' required to make it a mystery. Revelation in 'The Man that was Used Up' is used not to 'lift' the reader to a higher plane but to humble the reader's anticipation by revealing everything in a bathetic climax. What in 'Ligeia' is uncanny becomes in the satiric tale merely ludicrous. The narrator in 'Ligeia' begins by telling us: 'I cannot, for my soul, remember how, when or even precisely where, I first became acquainted with the Lady Ligeia. Long years have since elapsed, and my memory is feeble through much suffering. Or, perhaps I cannot *now* bring these points to mind'.[35]

All this we find again in the opening of 'The Man that was Used Up'—the vagueness of atmosphere, the loss of memory, the long lapse of time—but it is his use of hesitancy that produces the comic effect:

> I cannot just now remember when or where I first made the acquaintance of that truly fine looking fellow, Brevet Brigadier General John A.B.C. Smith. Some one *did* introduce me to the gentleman, I am sure — at some public meeting, I know very well—held about something of great importance, no doubt—at some place or other, I feel convinced—whose name I have unaccountably forgotten.[36]

Both characters make an extraordinary impression upon the two narrators. Of Ligeia one writes,

> in truth, the character of my beloved, her rare learning, her singular yet placid caste of beauty, and the thrilling eloquence of her low musical language, made their way into my heart by paces so steadily and stealthily progressive that they have been unnoticed and unknown.[37]

And this is matched by the comic narrator who comments of the object of his interest, 'there was something, as it were, remarkable—yes, *remarkable*, although this is but a feeble term to express my full meaning—about the entire individuality of the personage in question'.[38]

It is this 'individuality', or 'uniqueness' that constantly attracts the analytic gaze and that makes the narrator, in narrating the object of his analysis search beyond the object into its background. Thus, in both the serious work and its parody the principal characters have an aristocratic background. 'Yet', says one narrator, 'I believe that I met her first and most frequently in some large, old decaying city near the Rhine. Of her family—I have surely heard her speak. That it is of a remotely ancient date cannot be doubted'.[39] Of Brevet Brigadier General A.B.C. Smith the other narrator comments, 'there was an air *distingué* pervading the whole man, which spoke of high breeding and hinted at high birth'.[40]

So far the comic has run parallel to, yet not superseded in its excesses, the serious work. It is not until we delve deeper into the stories that, by comparison, certain differences become more marked. Hence, while both Ligeia's and Brevet Brigadier General A. B. C. Smith's eyes are described, it is the Brigadier General's legs which are brought next into focus rather than, as in 'Ligeia' the raven hair which is of so mysterious a nature. Thus, while Ligeia 'came and departed as a shadow', in 'The Man that was Used Up' the Brigadier General is literally a shadow of a man, a mechanical 'doll', whose 're-incarnation' is accomplished not by metempsychosis but by his butler helping him into all his various prostheses: 'a cork leg', a 'shoulder', 'breast', 'wig', 'teeth', and 'palate'.[41]

It is these differences between the serious work and the satiric counterpart which psychoanalysis too often levels out. There can be no difference for a certain psychoanalytic approach if the text is animated by 'serious' neurotic interests or if it is a comic parody as in 'The Man that was Used Up' when we are told by the narrator, 'I am constitutionally nervous—this, with me, is a family failing, and I can't help it. In especially, the slightest appearance of mystery—of any point I cannot exactly comprehend—puts me at once into a pitiable state of agitation'.[42]

At an essential point in Bonaparte's analysis of the psychological predisposition required to produce a work such as *Eureka* she sets her voice against Poe in a parody of his style in the form of a paraphrase. Bonaparte's parody is both breathless and revelatory. Mimicking Poe's axiomatic style in a series of rhetorical statements that Bonaparte declares are merely paraphrases of Poe's own words, she writes:

> And Poe, in the paranoid attack in which he composed *Eureka*, even goes so far as to deny his generic subordination as regards the Father and God. He is as great as God; he has existed from the beginning; like God, he is eternal. For who could admit, at some 'luminous point of his life of thought'—exactly the point which, as he says, he himself has reach!—who could understand or believe that anything exists *greater than his own soul?*'.[43]

Here is the crisis, the whirling centre of Poe's neurosis. Poe, for Bonaparte, sees himself as a unitary ego, and therefore a paranoid ego, a figure deluding himself in his autonomy. By exposing the delusion, by showing the shattered pieces of his 'real' ego, Bonaparte can reconstruct Poe in the symbolic framework of psychoanalysis. Subsequent critics writing on Poe have also used this stylistic method of dramatising Poe's statements, almost as if they were parts of Poe's conversation; Harry Levin is one:

> Other artists ... have likened the artist to a demiurge, and have stressed the analogy between the work and material creation. For Poe the relationship was no mere metaphor; it was a personal apothesis. *Eureka* is his heart-cry. 'I have found it' he breathlessly seems to announce. 'The secret of the universe, the burden of the mystery! Come, sit down upon a cloud with me, and I shall explain it all to you. Do you know who created the world? I did, just now'.[44]

Poe's paranoia declares itself in a denial of his ultimate subjection to 'God', and thereby a denial of his mortality, for, says Bonaparte, 'like God, he is eternal'. That Poe *does not* say this in *Eureka* is part of the complication caused by a parody which seems merely to be restating an argument from the analysed author, who 'even goes so far as'. The inclusion of quoted phrases only compounds a problem made worse by a 'mimicry' of Poe's grammatical style with its exclamations, hyphens and delayed climax. For who could admit at some 'luminous point of his life of thought'—exactly the point which, as he says, he himself has reached—who could understand or believe that anything exists 'greater than his own soul?'.[45]

By this parody Bonaparte allows herself to put a question into Poe's work. The question 'who could admit' is joined to an actual quote and thus a question supposedly asked by Poe is posed. The reader is now implicated as a participant within the struggle for mastery of the text between Poe and Bonaparte. If we, as readers, answer the question put by Bonaparte through Poe in the negative then we too are 'paranoid'. If we do not, then we realise by the dramatic example of parody Poe's neurotic tendency. Identification and transference loom up to re-structure Bonaparte's re-solution of Poe's philosophy.

Thus Bonaparte forces her own reading upon Poe in order to inscribe him within the analytic situation, now, as we have seen, as a double of the analysed itself in its form of parody. Michel Foucault sees this movement in the earliest novels of gothic terror, whereby the genre is immediately inhabited by its legitimate form *and* its satirical counterpart, each intertwining and encompassing the other. He writes:

> Yet these novels of terror are accompanied by an ironic movement which doubles and divides them, and which is not the result of historical repercussions or an effect of tedium. In a phenomenon quite rare in the history of literary language, satire in this instance is exactly contemporaneous with the situation it parodies. It is as if two twin and complementary languages were born at once from the same central source: one existing entirely in its naivity, the other within parody; one existing solely for the readers' eyes, the other moving from the readers' simple-minded fascination to the easy tricks of the writer. But in actuality, these two languages are more than simply contemporaneous; they lie within each other, share the same dwelling, constantly intertwine, forming a single verbal web and, as it were, a forked language that turns against itself from within, destroying itself in its own body, poisonous in its very density.[46]

With Michel Foucault's ambiguity of expression we see that in the relationship of parody to the serious work it satirises we find, 'one existing [but which one; parody or the serious work?] entirely in its naivity, the other [the serious work?] within parody'. As each in its rhetorical form enwraps the other, neither is separable and these 'two languages' do indeed 'lie within each other'. Bonaparte's sophisticated parody, as it becomes more sophisticated, becomes both more blatant and more 'naive'. Indeed Poe's texts exist both in their seriousness and as their own parodies. Bonaparte (re)writes Poe only to be rewritten herself when her text imitates that to which it is indebted: Edgar Allan Poe as the *subject under analysis*. There then follows the possibility of reconstituting the Bonaparte text through Poe's tales, as the analysis she provides curiously repeats their narrative pattern which is one that 'empties out' a body, followed by control and manipulation in order to reconstitute the body by a type of refilling process.

This scheme is only possible when the text invokes *another reality* in *addition* to the one experienced by the characters inhabiting the text. In Marie Bonaparte's text she invokes another reality by using psychoanalysis to explain Poe's *Eureka* not on its own terms but in terms of a peculiar psychological disposition on the part of its creator. The addition provides a place for both authority and correspondence.

The authority to whom Bonaparte addresses Poe's words is science with its 'high objective value'. The scientist may be an 'intuitive', says Bonaparte but unlike the artist 'the Keplers and Laplaces ... at the same time [employed] inductive and deductive methods ... to test their intuitions against the final arbiter, reality'.[47] This evidence from 'reality' allows the scientist such as Bonaparte to comment on the symbolism of one of Poe's tales (Bonaparte accepts *de facto* that it is symbolic) that 'as to the long and prominent rat's tail, that doubtless is an offshot of the *penis* which the child originally attributes to the mother'.[48] A passage which moves from the evidence of longness and prominence of the 'rat's tail' to the 'doubtless' assertion of its symbolic meaning in 'the penis' with its origination according to Bonaparte in the 'phallic' mother. Hence, Poe's symbolism is clearly translated.

Against this scientific image with its description, evidence, analysis and conclusion is placed Poe the artist with his 'deeply subjective complexes', which lead him to 'confound beauty and truth, intuition and knowledge, affirmation and proof'.[49] 'Like a true poet', says Bonaparte, 'Poe confounds provable theories with daydreams'.[50] Bonaparte continues, 'though, therefore, the manifest tale normally obeys the rules of logic, this deeper current is subject to other laws'.[51] Quite simply, it is these that authorise the analyst to deal with the text, these 'other laws' which require it to be brought under the 'rules of logic' by the analysing discourse. 'As we know', Bonaparte assures us, 'dream-states ... can be thoroughly consistent in certain delusional conditions'.[52] Science studies the conditions for the consistency of delusional states. But what happens when analysis doubles back upon itself as a parody of that which it analyses? What is the 'psychology' in such a textual manoeuvre?

Analysis as imitation becomes caricature as mimicry as the analyst is inscribed within the analysed's circle, the language produced being 'poisonous in its very density'. The critical procedure becomes 'uncanny' (as a repetition-compulsion) at the moment Bonaparte mimics what she seeks to undo. 'This assumption of the other person's characteristics', says R. D. Laing, 'may come to amount to an almost total impersonation of the other. The *hatred of the impersonation* becomes evident when the impersonation begins to turn into caricature'.[53] Bonaparte noted this very tendency in Poe as producing 'what amounted to a satirical comment on his Father through the medium of a compulsive caricature of him'.[54]

In this way Bonaparte becomes entangled in the very problem Freud warned his possible biographers against. 'It is true', says Freud, 'that the biographer does not want to depose his hero, but he does want to bring him nearer to us. That means, however, reducing the distance that separates him from us: it still tends in effect towards degradation'. Here the biography suffers the fate, according to Bonaparte, of all literature for, she emphasises, 'it must not be forgotten that though, on the surface, a literary work relates a manifestly coherent story, intertwined with it, and simultaneously, another and secret story is being told which, in fact, is the basic theme'.[55]

Indeed, this 'secret story' (the metapsychological structure of her relationship to Poe?) is working within Bonaparte's own text. I have already said that Bonaparte uses a certain narrative technique in order to refill Poe's texts with their meaning (contained ultimately in psychoanalytic concepts). To achieve this I have shown that Bonaparte 'ignores' (in order to reduce) the textuality of Poe's work so that her additional reality will reconstruct Poe as a biographical presence in his work. The analysed text is now doubly bound to its interpretation in that the interpretation attempts to show that the mechanisms operating in and upon the text's creation are *recoverable* at the end of the text as the text's *meaning*.

Yet, Bonaparte 'imitates' Poe. This imitation ignores, and is trapped within, Poe's own narrative technique. If Bonaparte's text 'repeats' Poe's text it is possible to use a fictional tale by Poe to analyse the discourse of analysis that Bonaparte employs. Procedure is then reversed. Bonaparte's text would find its 'meaning' in Poe's fictional technique; her reduction of Poe's texts to their author-persona would be set against Poe's reconstruction of Bonaparte as an analyst-persona operating within her own text. If we now turn to Poe's 'The Facts in the Case of M. Valdemar' it is possible to show that Poe's text anticipates the analyst-analysand relationship that operates between Bonaparte and Poe in Bonaparte's critical text.

Sandor Ferenczi, referring to a technique psychoanalysis was soon to abandon and yet always be haunted by, indicated that, 'the impression of a far reaching analogy between hypnosis and neurosis becomes strengthened to the point of a conviction of their inherent sameness as soon as one reflects that in both states unconscious ideational complexes determine the phenomena'.[56] Ferenczi continued,

> the unconscious mental forces of the "medium" appear as the real active agent, whereas the hypnotist, previously pictured as all powerful, has to content himself with the part of an object used by the unconscious of the apparently unresisting "medium" according to the latter's individual and temporary disposition'.[57]

In 'control' the 'hypnotist' achieves his control over the medium by surrendering to the 'medium' and allowing the 'medium' to speak *through* the hypnotist. It is exactly at this point that the 'medium' (the text under scrutiny by the analyst) is disrupted by its being filtered through the analyst whose neutrality becomes suspect when, as Ferenczi pointed out, his own 'unconscious ideational complexes' help to 'determine the phenomena'.

This is where Jacques Lacan reminds analysts of the force of the transference between analysed and analyst as it continues to have efficacy even in the analyst's 're-solution'. 'This example demonstrates indeed how an act of communication may give the impression at which theorists too often stop' says Lacan, 'of allowing in its transmission but a single meaning, as though the highly significant commentary into which he who understands integrates it, could become unperceived by him ... be considered null'.[58]

Once the 'medium' finds a voice through the hypnotist, and once the hypnotist is implicated in the voice the medium produces, then criticism takes on the force of both poetry *and* psychoanalysis. The emphasis then shifts from the medium to the hypnotist, within whom, and to whom, the 'message' of the medium is 'addressed'. 'It is the 'calm', 'quiet', 'evenly hovering' awareness best suited to the pursuit of one unconscious by another' says Philip Rieff, 'Baudelaire's demand that the poet should be hypnotist and somnambulist combined translates perfectly into Freud's demand upon the psychoanalyst'.[59] Poe 'fictionalised' this relationship in his tale 'The Facts in the Case of M. Valdemar'.

Poe's tale is concerned with the attempts of a mesmerist to put a subject under his influence at the point of death and thereby 'arrest the process'.[60] His tale begins with a pretence of realism, of scientific observation and reporting:

> Of course I shall not pretend to consider it any matter for wonder, that the extraordinary case of M. Valdemar has excited discussion. It would have been a miracle had it not—especially under the circumstances. Through the desire of all parties concerned, to keep the affair from the public, at least for the present, or until we had farther opportunities for investigation—through our endeavours to effect this—a garbled or exaggerated account made its way into society, and became the source of many unpleasant misrepresentations, and, very naturally, of a great deal of disbelief.[61]

As a 'garbled account' of the 'affair' made its way into the public arena, the narrator, in his desire 'to give the *facts*', is forced to enter his account of the 'investigations' to prevent 'disbelief'. Hence, the scientist with his desire for facts, reports his investigations where only a 'garbled account' existed, and in so doing strictly adheres to the injunctions of reality. Yet, at the same time, the events reported are 'extraordinary'; the facts of the fabulous are to be considered:

> It is now rendered necessary that I give the facts—as far as I comprehend them myself. They are, succinctly, these:

46

My attention, for the last three years, had been repeatedly drawn to the subject of Mesmerism; and, about nine months ago, it occurred to me, quite suddenly, that in the series of experiments made hitherto, there had been a very remarkable and most unaccountable omission:- no person had as yet been mesmerized in *articulo mortis*. It remained to be seen, first, whether, in such condition, there existed in the patient any susceptibility to the magnetic influence; secondly, whether, if any existed, it was impaired or increased by the condition; thirdly, to what extent, or for how long a period, the encroachments of Death might be arrested by the process.[62]

The narrator is to make an experiment that curiously has been 'omitted'. By doing so, the narrator will first see if a person can be 'mesmerized in *articulo mortis*, secondly if there existed any 'susceptibility' to mesmerism ('the magnetic influence'), and if the condition of the 'patient' 'impaired or increased' susceptibility, and lastly if the process might arrest 'Death'. The narrator finds his subject in the author M. Ernest Valdemar:

In looking around me for some subject by whose means I might test these particulars, I was brought to think of my friend, M. Ernest Valdemar, the well-known compiler of the 'Bibliotheca Forensica', and author (under the *nom de plume* of Issachar Marx) of the Polish versions of 'Wallenstein' and 'Gargantua'—M. Valdemar, who has resided principally at Harlaem, N.Y., since the year 1839, is (or was) particularly noticeable for the extreme spareness of his person—his lower limbs much resembling those of John Randolph; and, also, for the whiteness of his whiskers, in violent contrast to the blackness of his hair—the latter, in consequence, being very generally mistaken for a wig. His temperament was markedly nervous, and rendered him a good subject for mesmeric experiment.[63]

The subject for 'mesmeric experiment' is enwrapped in texts. As an author Valdemar appears under his *'nom de plume'* in the works he has translated, 'the Polish versions of "Wallenstein" and "Gargantua"'. As an author he is described in terms of white and black: paper and ink, 'for the whiteness of his whiskers, in violent contrast to the blackness of his hair' which because of the 'violent contrast' ... was 'generally mistaken for a wig'.[64] Equivocation then (in the artifice of his *nom de plume* and the artificiality of his wig), marks Poe's text from the outset, an equivocation that will occupy the relationship between hypnotist and medium.

Moreover, though Valdemar's temperament 'was markedly nervous', rendering him, 'a good subject for mesmeric experiment ... his will was at no period positively, or thoroughly, under my control and in regard to *clairvoyance*', the narrator, 'could accomplish with him nothing to be relied upon'.[65] The mesmeric subject will therefore find a certain latitude in his dealings with the mesmerist.

Having no 'relatives in America who would be likely to interfere' Valdemar gives his consent (*a written note*) to proceed.[66] The narrator begins soon afterwards. Again, as the experiment proceeds the text reminds us of its equivocation over its artificiality, for the narrator tells us that a certain 'Mr L–l was so kind to accede ... to take notes of all that occurred; and it is from his memoranda that what I [the narrator] have to relate is, for the most part, either condensed or copied *verbatim*'.[67] *Reporting* and *condensation* become the methods for narration. Meanwhile, the subject comes under the influence of the mesmerist/hypnotist, *through whom* the subject's mesmeric glance is thrown inward in expectation of a closer examination of the subject's 'soul'. 'At five minutes before eleven' the narrator tells us, 'I perceived unequivocal signs of the mesmeric influence. The glassy roll of the eyes was changed for that expression of uneasy *inward* examination which is never seen except in cases of sleep-walking, and which it is quite impossible to mistake'.[68] Instead of an inward narrative by the patient, the mesmerist now gives only a descriptive analysis of the patient's outward appearance:

> While I spoke, there came a marked change over the countenance of the sleep-waker. The eyes rolled themselves slowly open, the pupils disappearing upwardly; the skin generally assumed a cadaverous hue, resembling not so much parchment as white paper; and the circular hectic

spots which, hitherto, had been strongly defined in the centre of each cheek, *went out* at once. I use this expression, because the suddenness of their departure put me in mind of nothing so much as the extinguishment of a candle by a puff of the breath. The upper lip, at the same time, writhed itself away from the teeth, which it had previously covered completely; while the lower jaw fell with an audible jerk, leaving the mouth widely extended, and disclosing in full view the swollen and blackened tongue. I presume that no member of the party then present had been unaccustomed to death-bed horrors; but so hideous beyond conception was the appearance of M. Valdemar at this moment, that there was a general shrinking back from the region of the bed.[69]

At this point, the narrative changes from one in which experiment is part of observation of reality to one in which experiment is *directly responsible for a narrative of the fabulous*, 'I now feel that I have reached a point of this narrative at which every reader will be startled into positive disbelief. It is my business, however, simply to proceed'.[70]

The narrative of the expostulation of the experimenter now takes the form of the reply of the medium, a reply centred on the invocation of the voice of the now deceased Valdemar:

There was no longer the faintest sign of vitality in M. Valdemar; and concluding him to be dead, we were consigning him to the charge of the nurses, when a strong vibratory motion was observable in the tongue. This continued for perhaps a minute. At the expiration of this period, there issued from the distended and motionless jaws a voice—such as it would be madness in me to attempt describing. There are, indeed, two or three epithets which might be considered as applicable to it in part; I might say, for example, that the sound was harsh, and broken and hollow; but the hideous whole is indescribable, for the simple reason that no similar sounds have ever jarred upon the ear of humanity. There were two particulars, neverthe-less, which I thought then, and still think, might fairly be stated as characteristic of the intonation—as well adapted to convey some idea of its unearthly peculiarity. In the first place, the voice seemed to reach our ears—at least mine—from a vast distance, or from some deep cavern within the earth. In the second place, it impressed me (I fear, indeed, that it will be impossible to make myself comprehended) as gelatinous or glutinous matters impress the sense of touch.[71]

The 'indescribable' voice is now no longer the voice of the living Valdemar but a 'dead' voice intoned *through the body* of Valdemar who speaks the 'biologically' impossible sentence 'I *have been* sleeping—and now—now—*I am dead*'.[72] Roland Barthes comments upon 'the turning of the metaphorical into the literal', by saying:

> It is in effect banal to utter the sentence 'I am dead': it is what is said by the woman who has been shopping all afternoon ... the turning of the metaphorical into the literal, precisely for this metaphor, is impossible: the enunciation 'I am dead', is literally foreclosed (whereas 'I sleep' remained literally possible in the field of hypnotic sleep). It is, then, if you like a scandal of language which is in question.[73]

Valdemar speaks (but is 'dead') in reply to the question previously put by the narrator, in a 'voice' that emanates neither from the body of the deceased nor the mesmerist but the very body of the text itself, like a ventriloquist and his dummy. The voice uncannily 'doubles' its original possessor (now possessed by it) and *mimics* the articulation of the human voice: 'I have spoken both of "sound" and of "voice". I mean to say that the sound was one of distinct—of even wonderfully, thrillingly distinct—syllabification. M. Valdemar spoke—obviously [and yet he is dead] in reply to the question I had propounded to him a few minutes before'.[74]

Valdemar's rapport is only with the mesmerist and 'to queries put to him by any other person than myself he seemed utterly insensible—although I endeavoured to place each member of the company in mesmeric rapport with him'.[75] Indeed, Valdemar's relationship to death and unreality is equivalent to, as the double of, the narrator's relationship with life and reality.

The narrator's rapport with Valdemar finds its outlet in Valdemar's speech, which automatically repeats its statement over its own death, even though by its being able to speak, and by the narrator's reporting that 'death had been arrested', its very presence equivocates over life and death in the tale.[76] It is the form of reply which seems to animate a 'dead' content: the meaning of death.

The narrator's last question directly to which the reply is addressed, asks finally, 'M. Valdemar, can you explain to us what are your feelings or wishes now?'[77] From which the final crisis is precipitated. Valdemar's voice animated into 'life' *only when spoken to*, screams, 'For God's sake!—quick!—quick!—put me to sleep—or, quick!—waken me!—quick!—*I say to you that I am dead*!'.[78] Though he knows his state is death, Valdemar demands both sleep and waking, neither being the true state to match his reiterated assertion. The mesmerist, mistaken as to the subject's true state, though evidence (*the* evidence) is apparent in the dissolution of the body, believes he can waken Valdemar:

> I was thoroughly unnerved, and for an instant remained undecided what to do. At first I made an endeavour to re-compose the patient; but, failing in this through total abeyance of the will, I retraced my steps and as earnestly struggled to awaken him. In this attempt I soon saw that I should be successful—or at least I soon fancied that my success would be complete—and I am sure that all in the room were prepared to see the patient awaken.[79]

How is this tale—a parody of scientific experiment and analysis as well as a supremely fictional narrative of the fabulous—related to Bonaparte's essay? How does this tale of the manipulation of a body anticipate her work? If we look at Poe's various phrases to describe the relationship of medium to mesmerist/hypnotist we see the mechanism whereby Bonaparte 'resurrects' Poe.

We have seen in the application of Marie Bonaparte's critique of Poe an attempt to give the facts of Poe's life and works instead of the 'garbled account' as Poe says which 'served to keep ignorant...for almost a century his readers'. To do this Bonaparte used 'the laws revealed by Freud' to prevent 'disbelief'.

The experiment which she attempted tried to reveal the pathology of a great (though 'morbid') writer, whose work is 'extra-ordinary'. Bonaparte's experiment attempts to throw a light upon the facts behind the fabulous.

Firstly, she makes this attempt to see if Poe's biographical motivations can be re-examined even though he is dead (actually in *articulo mortis* as his work is still read and criticised). Having done so she will see if this morbid pathology is susceptible to the 'magnetic influence' of psychoanalysis, and if so whether this 'new' method can 'revive' Poe and arrest his 'death'. As with Valdemar's history the whole is enwrapped in a text. Poe's 'neurosis', which so well understands the influences of electricity, makes him the ideal subject for the experiment. Since Poe has 'no relatives in America who would be likely to interfere' Bonaparte begins.

Bonaparte's influence makes ready Poe's '*inward* examination', yet Bonaparte, as we have seen, can achieve little in regard of 'clairvoyance' and cannot always get the subject 'under … control'. A mixture of reporting and 'condensation' allowed Bonaparte to re-solve her analysis as the Poe narrator resolved his. Before being filled with psychoanalysis, Poe's texts like Valdemar begin to empty out, 'the emaciation was so extreme that the skin had been broken through … his expectoration was excessive'.[80] The symptomatic body from *whose depths* the meaning of the texts will *flow* is dispensed with by the analyst.

It is this flow of meaning which is so important in the 're-solution' of the analyst's problem of interpretation. What flows from Valdemar's body is waste, what flows from Valdemar's 'voice' is death.

In Poe's 'Valdemar', the meaning of each is not explored, it is the reaction of life upon death that disturbs the narration, an attempt to beget life on death. Interestingly this birth metaphor is expressly present in the tale. 'Nine months ago' the narrator becomes interested in the experiment, two months into that nine the narrator receives his note from Valdemar and at the end of nine months, which is the end of the tale, Valdemar gives birth in death:

As I rapidly made the mesmeric passes, amid ejaculations of 'dead! dead!' absolutely *bursting* from the tongue and not from the lips of the sufferer, his whole frame at once—within the space of a single minute, or even less, shrunk—crumbled—absolutely *rotted* away beneath my hands. Upon the bed, before that whole company, there lay a nearly liquid mass of loathsome—of detestable putridity.[81]

Upon the bed nothing but putridity remains, meaning has not been born, no interpretation offered, the 'afterbirth' of meaning remains where meaning has not appeared. The 'rapport' between analyst and analysed, hypnotist and medium has not brought about the expected results but, instead, presents a counterfeit of life, through which 'death' has been infused momentarily with 'ejaculations of dead! dead! absolutely *bursting* from the tongue'.[82]

The medium speaks in order to refuse to speak, the hypnotist speaks in order to articulate via the text that *refusal* and that *submission* which will always open it up to meaning (the 'passive body). André Green remarks:

> The work of art is handed over to the analyst . . . it cannot reveal the state of its functioning through the operation that consists in analysing by free association—that is to say, by providing material that reveals its nature in the very act by which it makes itself known. It does not possess any of the resources that make analysis bearable: that of going back on what one has said, rejecting the intolerable connection at the moment when it presents itself, putting off the moment of an emerging awareness, even denying, by one of the many ways available to the analysand, the correctness of an interpretation or the obviousness of some truth brought by repetition to the front of the stage and needing to be deciphered. The work remains obstinately mute, closed in upon itself, without defences against the treatment that the analyst may be tempted to subject it to.[83]

Thus, as Joseph Breuer remarks, 'in dreams we find ourselves talking to a dead person without remembering that he is dead'.[84] Poe appears as the subject 'medium' of Bonaparte's tale, while as the character to whom he will address himself Bonaparte appears as the character of the narrator-hypnotist-analyst.

In looking at Marie Bonaparte's psychobiography I have concentrated attention upon the problems of technical, stylistic and conceptual 'doubling' as they are produced by an over-confident metalanguage in search of cause and effect and grounded in its own image of what science should be and what shape the practice of a scientist should take.

While Bonaparte's text gains many intelligent insights, and closely reads both Poe and Freud, it is the 'secret story' of translation and transference, from one author to another through one discourse to another, that has animated this study. Psychoanalytic practice, through its concepts, allows Marie Bonaparte to read Poe and us to read Bonaparte reading Poe. Bonaparte uses psychoanalysis as a body of applied concepts whereas we have tried to find the psychoanalytic concepts operating in her text *as technique*. Psychoanalysis allows us to re-read Poe in a very different way from Bonaparte though the same concepts are used.

Psychoanalysis as a practice is activated by Bonaparte's text as it operates on Edgar Allan Poe, but, at the same time, lives beyond Bonaparte in a textually produced mesh of interwoven theory and practice which she has incorporated into her own discourse. At the same moment as she begins to analyse the Poe texts as texts they are both made available again to us through psychoanalysis and make available the very applied discourse to which they are subjected. The requirement of an analysing discourse that it be 'invisible' (silent, yet, loquacious: the 'objective' style) is denied as the discourse exposes itself through the text it uses for its appropriation. We have seen how Bonaparte both 'opens up' and absorbs the Poe texts while *they* re-interpret the techniques of her interpretation. In Freud we can see how this equates with the workings of the psyche:

> Such symptoms participate in the ego from the very beginning, since they fulfill a requirement of the super-ego, while on the other hand they represent positions occupied by the repressed and points at which an irruption has been made by it into the ego—organization. They are a kind of frontier-station.... The ego now proceeds to behave as

54

though it recognized that the symptom had come to stay and that the only thing to do was to accept the situation in good part and draw as much advantage from it as possible. It makes an adaption to the symptom—to this piece of the internal world which is alien to it—just as it normally does to the real external world. It can always find plenty of opportunities for doing so.... In this way the symptom gradually comes to be the representative of important interests; it is found to be useful in asserting the position of the self and becomes more and more closely merged within the ego and more and more indispensable to it.[85]

Thus Poe's ideas, initially antithetical to Bonaparte, are absorbed into the discourse of her analysis so that by only signifying through that discourse they come to be the very example with which the discourse will justify itself. Poe's texts finally become the example which validates the method.

4

Artaud, Infection, the Body, Nothingness

The Tudor theatre and the problem of theatrical meaning

November 1581 brought this instruction from the Privy Council to the good Aldermen of the City of London:

> After our hartie commendations. Whereas for auoyding the increase of infection within your citie this last somer yow receaued order from vs for the restrainte of plaies vntill Mighelmas last. For that (thankes be to god) the sicknesse is very well seised and not likely in this time of the yeare to increase; Tendering the releife of theis poore men the players and their redinesse with conuenient matters for her highnes solace this next Christmas, which cannot be without their vsuall exercise therein; We haue therefore thought good to requier yowe forethwith to suffer them to vse such plaies in such sort and vsuall places as hath ben heretofore accustomed, hauing carefull regard for continuance of such quiet orders in the playeng places as tofore yowe haue had. And thus we bidd yowe hartelie farewell from the Courte at Whitehall.[1]

Restraint of the theatre brings in its wake a restraining and reduction of disease—'plaies' are restored after the therapy of an absence, restored and contained within the 'vsual places as hath ben heretofore accustomed'; containment follows partial purgation.

Plague brought by the strolling players of Tudor times threatens social order as the players themselves threaten political order; they must be contained because they are disorderly. Here is another instruction, this time dated almost twenty years previously, in February 1564:

> Mr. Calfhill this mornynge shewed me your letter to him, wherin ye wishe some politike orders to be devised agaynste Infection. I thinke it verie necessarie, and wille doo myne endevour bothe by exhortation, and otherwise. I was readye to crave your helpe for that purpose afore, as one nott vnmyndefulle of the parishe.
>
> By searche I doo perceive, thatt ther is no one thinge off late is more lyke to have renewed this contagion, then the practise off an idle sorte off people, which have ben infamouse in all goode common weales: I meane these Histriones, common playours; who now daylye, butt speciallye on holydayes, sett vp bylles, whervnto the youthe resorteth excessively, & ther taketh infection: besydes that goddes worde by theyr impure mowthes is prophaned, and turned into scoffes; for remedie wheroff in my jugement ye shulde do verie well to be a meane, that a proclamation wer sette furthe to inhibitte all playes for one whole yeare (and iff itt wer for ever, it wer nott amisse) within the Cittie, or 3.myles compasse, vpon paynes aswell to the playours, as to the owners off the howses, wher they playe theyr lewde enterludes.[2]

Here 'politike orders' need to be devised to contain the 'infection' and protect the 'parishe'. 'Contagion' comes with those 'idle sorte off people ... common playours'. Through these players' extravagances, through their acts of fiction, the 'youth' of the parish catch the contagion of immorality. Indeed, these very players are attacked for profaning 'goddes worde'. Thus, to the Bishop of London, Edmund Grindal, who sent this instruction, the very act of expression, of the players breathing out their spoken words, infects the audience, overturns morality, defies God and destroys order; God's moral law and the covenant of state and church are challenged by the fiction of players. Plague is accounted for not by a theory of virology but by a theory of corrupted expression, an expression that turns youth away from the proper expression of the pulpit and the orderly expression of those that guard the political law. Theatre is a religious problem precisely because it is a political problem; one whose treatment centres upon containment, exclusion and banishment in order to avoid outbreaks and the breakdown of government both local and national. Hence, in London increasingly frequent epidemics of plague are interpreted as God's vengeance for the 'withdrawinge of the Queenes Maiesties subjectes from dyvyne service on Sonndaies and hollydayes', to the 'inordynate havntynge of greate multitudes of people ... to playes, enterludes, and shewes'.[3]

Already, through a choice quirk of language, the withdrawal of the monarch's subjects to plays and from the church is said to bring the vengeance of a God who leaves these audiences spiritually 'dead' 'haunting' plays in their 'multitudes'. Plague comes as an interpretable 'sign': plays are sinful, sin is corruption, corruption is plague, plague kills and these people are the very emblem of death, a collective memento mori for the righteous who do go to church. Political order is threatened by 'ghosts'. Plague becomes the metaphor for an age obsessed with religion, politics and death; illness speaks for the extremes of a human consciousness aware of its age and its temper, it becomes more than a figurative expression and becomes configurative and bodies forth that age's sensibility not merely metaphorically but literally.[4]

Artaud finds this alliance of plague and theatre, understands its implications, writes *Theatre and the Plague*.[5] What does Artaud relate but an anecdote preserved in a town's archives of 1720. The town is Cagliari (mistranslated in the English edition as Caligari, whose name comes to speak in quite another place as the masterpiece of the German cinema, in which a somnabulist is put under the influence of a daemonic manipulator, a manipulator who infects and disrupts the 'ficticious' world of dream and makes it literal). So too, in 1720, in Cagliari, Sardinia.

The Sardinian Viceroy has a vivid and terrifying dream in which a ship, the 'Grand-Saint-Antoine' brings plague to the shores of his country. The ship named after the saint assailed by his own dementia, externalised and projected, returning to punish and destroy him, that ship carries a terrible punishment aboard: the Plague. This is what Artaud tells us the Viceroy dreamed:

Society's barriers became fluid with the effects of the scourge. Order disappeared. He witnessed the subversion of all morality, the breakdown of all psychology, heard his lacerated, utterly routed bodily fluids murmur within him in a giddy wasting away of matter, they grew heavy and were then gradually transformed into carbon. Was it too late to ward off the scourge? Although organically destroyed, crushed, extirpated, his very bones consumed, he knew one does not die in dreams, that our will-power even operates *ad absurdum*, even denying what is possible, in a kind of metamorphosis of lies reborn as truth.[6]

Assaulted by the plague, the body of the dreamer, of the representative of law and order, is broken down and becomes fluid, order disappears in his body as 'society's barriers' break down. Figuratively, but no less powerfully, the body of the ruler, identified in correspondent terms with that which he rules, is disorganised and destroyed. Nevertheless, the Viceroy, left with only will-power to force himself back to wakefulness, fights the dream, fights to avoid *not* waking up and really dying in his dream. For what does it mean to die in a dream, if we are not to interpret it as a mere preoccupation with sexual innuendo? It means precisely to enter the world of dream, to lose contact with the waking state, to let go into a region no one can return from sanely, for sanity is wakefulness.

The Viceroy acknowledges this. A dream is a fiction, fiction destroys only the fictional, fiction does not enter 'real' life. But this dream is a true portent. A real ship approaches—this very ship. Thus, the dream of the Viceroy contains no metaphoric message, no allegorical or symbolic weight, its presence marks the break off of the metaphoric and the beginning of the literal. Fiction, in the Viceroy's dream, precedes fate like a herald; fiction opens a space for the factual to enter, dressed as *that* fiction. As such, an age's myths become its living space, not metaphoric symbols. Not descriptions or definitions, or classifications, these mythic entities are the space in which we act, and from which we act. We are directed by them and gain their power by our desire to call them descriptive; this ship, this dream, determine the actions of the wakeful Viceroy, they stand guardian over his actions.

Here then, the Viceroy becomes a character in his own narrative, the dream narrative fixes and directs the living man, the dream touching and becoming objectified in biology and as it does so the dream—a dream placed inside temporal time but standing outside of it (it is a prophesy, an unveiling of a future *already* happening)—takes over historical time and enters the psyche of an eighteenth-century prince. The Viceroy cannot escape this prophesy, in it he wastes away under a subversion of 'morality' and a 'breakdown of all psychology'. Fiction empties and refills the Viceroy's psyche with itself—it literalises itself and externalises itself as a threat—yet it lurks within the systems of state and those of the biological organism. Awake, the Viceroy cannot escape the contagion of the dream and for a time his life becomes a literal nightmare. However, so potent is the dream that it appears to corrupt the Viceroy's mind, turning him from benign ruler into tyrannical despot. To his people the Viceroy, defined hitherto by Artaud as a man marked by the role expected of his title, begins to act as a tyrant and a 'fool' giving 'an order thought raving mad, absurd, stupid and despotic both by his subjects and his suite'.[7] Sensitivity, social concern and intelligence are the virtues that help the Viceroy maintain a plague-free city, but they disguise themselves as despotism, stupidity and insanity; the guardian of order adopts a mask, becomes *other than he is* to be more like he is, (or should we say 'was'): a Viceroy. The dream-ship guarantees the Viceroy's sanity even as it jeopardises that sanity.

The Viceroy *maintains* his sanity disguised by *insane* action, for 'this communication between Saint-Remys and the plague, though of sufficient intensity to release imagery in his dreams, was after all, not powerful enough to infect him with the disease'.[8] By a *psychic infection* the Viceroy maintains his immunity. And it is here that Artaud in his description of the disease would wish most radically to diverge from medical science: 'I think', he says, 'one might agree on the idea of the disease as a kind of psychic entity, not carried by a virus'.[9]

Nevertheless, this psychic infection manifests itself on the body of the victim, tattooing the body with its hieroglyphs, and these hieroglyphs unite the body of man with the body of the cosmos: microcosm becomes macrocosm.

These blisters are surrounded by rings, the outer one, just like Saturn's ring at maximum radiance, indicating the outer edge of the bubo.

The body is streaked with them. Just as volcanoes have their own chosen locations on earth, the bubos have their own chosen spots over the expanse of the human body. Bubos appear around the anus, under the armpits, at those precious places where the active glands steadily carry out their functions, and through these bubos the anatomy discharges either its inner putrefaction, or in other cases, life itself. A violent burning sensation localised in one spot, more often than not indicates that the life force has lost none of its strength and that abatement of the sickness or even a cure may be possible. Like silent rage, the most terrible plague is one that does not disclose its symptoms.[10]

The body, psychosomatically, releases the message of the plague. But this message is withheld at the same time. What is witnessed on the body is nowhere acknowledged by the essence of the plague—that is withdrawn 'like silent rage'. However, the body displays emblematically the presence of plague, the body is possessed by one passion, plague, and thus takes on the age-old representational form of the medieval 'humour'. The body then becomes allegorised, disengaged from the fullness of life, operating under the pressure of one daemonic impulse: the impulse to empty itself into its surroundings and die. However, even this is disguised: 'the life force [seems to have] lost none of its strength'. At that moment the body acknowledges death, death disguised as life. Plague as a force on the moral plain leaves its victims living ghosts witnessed 'haunting' the playhouses of Tudor England. The 'life force', as Artaud describes it, covers up the fact that death is already in charge of the victim: death directs life.

Plague, as this death, retains the occulted nature of its (non)presence. As Artaud's 'psychic entity' plague makes of the interior body a kind of ectoplasmic soup which by natural means, but from supernatural origin, exudes itself into exteriority—opening out to be read as a form of expression, of a corrupted expression preceded by 'that hugely swollen panting tongue', which turns, 'first white, then red, then black... heralding unprecedented organic disturbances'.[11] God's word, the prophesy of corruption, becomes literal corruption and opens itself for interpretation by the righteous. This is the writing that crosses and recrosses the body of the prisoner in Kafka's *Penal Settlement*, an external writing machine under pressure of which the body of the prisoner transmits to the psyche of the prisoner the cause of his punishment:

> The Harrow is the instrument for the actual execution of the sentence ... he'll [the prisoner] learn it corporally on his person ... the long needle does the writing, and the short needle sprays a jet of water to wash away the blood and keep the inscription clean ... it's no calligraphy for school children ... the man [the prisoner] ... begins to understand the inscription, he purses his mouth as if he were listening. You have seen how hard it is to decipher the script with one's eyes; but our man deciphers it with his wounds.[12]

While in Kafka this punishment works toward an interior recognition, in Artaud this recognition is *always* interiorised, in the rehearsed space of a psyche (is this why Artaud wrote so little actual theatre?). Yet, both Kafka's punishment and Artaud's plague keep the secret of their power and do not exhibit it. This power is that of a psychic empathy between the writing and that upon which it writes: the soul. The secret is recognised silently by an inner correspondence. Whereas the Viceroy escapes the writing, although unwillingly undergoing its influence, the captain of Kafka's story wills the machine to inscribe his righteousness, his sense of an older and clearer order, on his body; the machine breaks down, order collapses, the words become merely illegible, the victim dies in torment on his own internal machine of the law. The law writing itself in plague victims discloses its representatives but hides itself; autopsy reveals nothing, for 'once open, a plague victim's body exhibits no venom'.[13] Thus, hidden behind the visible, the empty body of the victim, or the vitrified body of the victim reveals *nothing*. Here the body is inhabited by nothing and the essence of nothingness thus usurps the space of a living being. And this nothingness inhabits and overcomes those very organs that are involved with expression. Artaud continues, 'the only two organs really affected ... the brain and the lungs, are both dependent on consciousness or the will'.[14] And, yet, this nothingness which takes over the very will of the victim expresses itself as something, the body gives 'birth' to spectacle:

> The scum of the populace, immunised so it seems by their frantic greed, enter the open houses and help themselves to riches they know will serve no purpose or profit. At this point, theatre establishes itself....
>
> The remaining survivors go berserk; the virtuous and obedient son kills his father, the continent sodomise their kin. The lewd become chaste. The miser chucks handfuls of his gold out of the windows, the Soldier Hero sets fire to the town he had formerly risked his life to save. Dandies deck themselves out and stroll among the charnel-houses. Neither a concept of lack of sanctions nor one of imminent death are enough to motivate such pointlessly absurd acts among people who did not believe death could end anything. How else can we explain that upsurge of erotic fever among the recovered victims who, instead of escaping, stay behind, seeking out and snatching sinful pleasure from the dying or even the dead, half crushed under the pile of corpses where chance had lodged them.[15]

Antonin Artaud recognises what Edmund Grindal, Tudor Bishop of London understood—that theatre becomes a spectacle which cannot be contained, releasing latent energies, which expend themselves in acts of violent eroticism and absurdity; order is overturned under pressure from the inner nothingness now released—audience and actor are established but unconfirmed as to who is who. Artaud's manifesto of theatre is a manifesto dedicated to a theatre based upon the 'draining of abcesses'.[16] This cathartic theatre is a conscious return, says Artaud, to the tragic qualities of those Elizabethan and Jacobean plays such as Tis Pity She's a Whore which 'return the mind to the origins of its inner struggles', struggles which break through in theatrical performance to overwhelm, for the time of a play, the order which contains it and the knowledge which produces and accommodates that order; eroticism, knowledge and order find their 'unconscious' in theatre.[17]

5

King Lear: Deviation, Sexuality and the Conception of Nothing

Recent feminist criticism has returned to an interest in Elizabethan and Jacobean studies, concentrating especially upon Shakespeare. One group of critics tell us that in *King Lear* and elsewhere the extent to which Shakespeare aligns himself with patriarchy, merely portrays it, or deliberately criticises it 'remains a complex and open question, one that feminist criticism is aptly suited to address'.[1]

From this general statement some feminists have begun to deal with sexuality and its significance in Jacobean thought and its relationship to gender relationships. One critic, therefore, points out that for the Jacobean world female sexuality is one 'mythic source of power, an archetypal symbol that arouses both love and loathing in the male'.[2] This concern with the relationship of sexuality and power has led another feminist to try and identify 'significant femaleness' and 'significant maleness' in the Elizabethan psyche and to talk of a 'sexual obsession' at the time'.[3]

While all these critics identify a set of problems related to sexuality and power they do not attempt to consider this 'crisis' of identification in its relationship with a concept of knowledge *and* of textuality. This chapter is an attempt to put this debate in a certain perspective and also to take it to wider and further conclusions; conclusions concerned with the identification of, and productive forces behind, a concept of 'meaning' and 'significance'.

'Nothing will come of nothing'; *Lear* is a play that is conditioned by nothingness. It is, indeed, about having nothing to say or, more precisely, about the problem of the 'never-said', the 'thingness' or the presence in *Lear* of the 'never-to-be-articulated' dialogue and its subsequent and consequent providing of meaning. Initially, the answer to the problem of the 'never-said' is reasonably straightforward. Much of the play is filled with riddles and these are posed most often by the Fool, Lear's companion. It is necessary to go through the play and try to reconstruct the problem of nothingness that takes shape through the posing of riddles, and indeed through much else. Something has gone peculiarly out of synchronisation.

The play begins with a conversation between Gloucester and Kent, at which point Edmund enters. The initial two dozen lines are concerned with *breeding*, a pun on birth and the subsequent status it bestows. Unlike Edgar, Edmund is not a son 'by order of law' (1.i.18); his 'acknowledgement' is not that of an heir but that of a bastard. Now, at least three things are important here. The first is simply that, being born on the wrong side of wedlock, Edmund's conception brings 'good sport'. In other words illegitimate sexual activity is more fun than the legitimate sort sanctioned by law and noticeably under the *public* domain of social functions. Edmund is the result of *private* pleasure. Secondly, as a bastard Edmund has no rights, he is, along with the fool and the madman, a *deviation*, although admittedly with no particular dishonour. However, he is not the legitimate heir and therefore without prospect. He is *socially a nothing*, a nothing which his very presence proclaims; he is, as Gloucester says the product of a 'fault' (1.i.15). However, lurking in this density is one more problem. To Gloucester's comments on Edmund's paternity Kent replies 'I cannot conceive you' (1.i.11). The quibble on 'conceive' makes of the word a pun the direction of which splits in two ways. Obviously it means Kent does not fully understand Gloucester, yet, couched in these copulatory terms, it refers to the sexual roles of male and female in this play. Kent's seemingly casual conceit alerts us to the fact that issues of birth, paternity and filial duty are central to the play. Sexual roles are reversed in this play so that Kent's words point to the feminising of the men in the play. Through the feminising of their men, the women do not give them female sexual functions but make them *impotent*. We shall see this more fully later.

Moreover, the reference also brings in the idea of giving birth to meaning, the pregnant statement that contains within it a certain truth. As we have seen Kent cannot 'conceive' (1.i.11).

When Lear enters the play he immediately announces his 'darker purpose' in which he shall 'unburthen'd crawl towards death' (1.i.40). However, Lear is king. This abdication of his role as king strips him both of his status and of his manhood. Lear, in the order of the universe *must* be king and fulfil his role as king to be a *man*. To abdicate responsibility for one negates the other. Thus, 'unburthen'd' Lear becomes 'nothing' right at the start of the play. However, he survives throughout the action: he has a presence. Lear too becomes a deviation: a king who willingly and against divine ordination abdicates his *throne*. Lear's embarrassing position is that of the nothing with a presence, he becomes a 'ghost' haunting his daughters. It is his giving of his kingdom to his daughters which most dishonours this ghost. For Lear gives his power to two women who thirst for that power and in so doing problematise their relationship as wives to their respective dukes. Moreover, all the supposed sins of Eve hang about them; they are lecherous in their regard for Edmund, they are hungry to rule despite their husbands, they are jealous, and they are dissimulators toward their father in their courtier-like approach. They are, unlike Cordelia, *sophisticated*. It is the sophistication that enables them finally to usurp the place of the men in the ruling of a harmonious country. When women, the 'nothings' of the aristocratic marriage (remembering the Duke of Burgundy 'barters' for Cordelia like an object of commerce—'But now her price is fallen' says Lear (1.i.196)), take over then nothingness replaces the masculine 'somethingness' and the harmony of the universe becomes rebellious; family strife, filial strife, marriage strife all prefigure civil war and invasion.

This brings us to the three speeches that characterise this scene. Those of the two sisters Goneril and Regan and those of Cordelia and Lear. As Lear states 'now we will divest us both of rule, interest of territory, cares of state' (I.i.48–9) as he asks the three sisters for their protestations of love. In clearly giving voice to that which cannot be articulated (the emotion of love) both Goneril and Regan say in their speeches precisely nothing or, to be more clear, they mean the negation of what they say. Goneril first:

Sir, I love you more than words can wield the matter;
Dearer than eyesight, space and liberty;
Beyond what can be valued rich or rare;
No less than life, with grace, health, beauty, honour;
As much as child e'er loved or father found;
A love that makes breath poor and speech unable;
Beyond all manner of so much I love you. (I.i.54–60)

Goneril's speech contains two elements (both belonging, as Cordelia says, to that 'glib and oily art. ... To speak and purpose not' (I.i.223–5)). The first is the cataloguing contained in all panegyric. Goneril piles up superlatives to prove that even in this hyperbolic context love is beyond compare: the ultimate superlative greater than these; but first she carefully names them all, all the way from 'eyesight' to 'honour'. The second element in her speech is that all these words, which like a good flatterer she does not omit to utter, are useless to name her love. 'More', she says, 'than word can wield the matter. ... A love that makes breath poor and speech unable'. What can be said about what cannot be named asks Goneril and then in a volume of 'hot air' she says it. The more she speaks the less her love equals anything. It does not evaporate, it was never there. Regan, to outdo her sister in praise says, 'I find she names my very deed of love' (I.i.70). Obviously there is heavy irony here. Her sister names a 'deed' which quibbles on a covenant in law which does not (for her) exist: the universal law of love that bonds daughter to father. The two sisters tell their father what is not lawful: *a lie, the negation that usurps the positive space taken up by true words*.

Then Lear turns to Cordelia. 'Speak' says he, 'nothing my Lord', says she (I.i.85–6). 'Nothing?' asks Lear. 'Nothing' is the reply. (I.i.88). 'Nothing will come of nothing: speak again' (I.i.89). But Cordelia's truth, the real love she feels, is unutterable. Her 'bond' (I.i.92) to her father is lawful, is true, is positive, but is rejected in favour of the false 'deed' of the two other sisters. The word 'nothing' echoes through the play as does the storm. Lear mistakes Cordelia's nothing which is true and positive for falseness and negation. He recognises unknowingly that from nothingness only barrenness follows, but fails to recognise that out of Cordelia's nothingness true meaning is articulated. Ecclesiasticus says 'the heart of fools is in their mouth: but the mouth of the wise is in their hearts' (21:26). Cordelia's mouth, *displaced* as it were, makes her *a deviant by being silent*. Her mouth wrongly placed for court flattery is nevertheless correctly placed for the silence that *is* truth although Lear mistakes silence for nothingness. By this silence through the word 'nothing' the play takes up deeply ethical and moral issues. On a stylistic level it gives space to a word that has no substance (the word *nothing*) and so stylistically nothingness again takes up space and by so doing displaces 'silence' for Cordelia does not stay silent but utters the word 'nothing' in its place. Thus, Cordelia reverses the meaning of what she intends her father to understand. Lear replies to the logic of Cordelia's following argument:

> *Lear*: So young, and so untender?
> *Cord*: So young, my lord, and true.
> *Lear*: Let it be so; thy truth then by thy dower (1.i.105–7)[4]

Mirroring this major scene is the minor scene in which Edmund rails against legitimacy, rejecting both brother and father. Gloucester enters to be tricked by Edmund over the letter Edmund has forged. 'What paper were you reading' asks Gloucester (I.ii.30). 'Nothing' replies Edmund (I.ii.31). Gloucester retorts with 'the quality of nothing hath not such need to hide itself. Let's see; come; if it be nothing, I shall not need spectacles' (I.ii.33–5).

Stylistically, Gloucester recalls Lear. But Edmund is technically correct when he says he has nothing, although quite obviously he dissimulates, for Edmund's 'something', the letter, *is itself* a forgery: a nothing. Edmund's letter *hides* the truth of itself (for it is a lie) by being exposed to Gloucester. Edmund's letter proves that the light of day hides the truth and that paradoxically darkness, silence and blindness reveal truth. Edmund tricks his father by exposing his lie. Thus Edmund invokes a paradox: to expose in the terms of the play is to conceal. Through two major modes of communication, first speech and then letter writing, first the sisters and then Edmund use communication to communicate non-meaning and the negation of communication, the end result of which should be some sort of understanding.

From the area of non-meaning the play moves easily into the area of non-sense through the lyrics of the fool and the madman. This too is prefigured in the early stages of the play by Kent when he asks Lear what the king will do when 'Lear is mad' (I.i.145). Indeed the bodily senses have already been deceived so that the mind is left defenceless. Eyes already deceive, appearances are false. Edmund's insistence that Gloucester will by an 'auricular assurance' know Edgar to be false is itself a further instance of deception.

Characteristically, Gloucester puts this sad affair down to a defect in Nature, 'these late eclipses' (I.ii.100) as he tells us of a recent solar phenomenon, in which, of course, the sun's light is blotted out leaving darkness and the nothingness of a black disc in the sky. Under such portents the human rebels as a mirror image. Cosmic disorder underpins and mirrors 'treason; and the bond crack'd between son and father' (I.ii.105–6) while human strife suffers under the 'prediction' (I.ii.107) of heaven. Interestingly, amid the catalogue of reversal and 'hollowness' (I.ii.110), Edmund is promised by Gloucester, 'Find out this villain [referring to Edgar]...it shall lose thee nothing' (I.ii.111–12). Gloucester's *son* becomes 'eclipsed'.

After Gloucester's rage against the times in which he lives, Edmund mirrors his speech by one which places man's misfortunes squarely upon himself. The two speeches *mirroring* and *reversing* each other cancel one another out in a grand swagger of style and in so doing remove the cosmic level from the action. Unable to interfere in man's tragedy, the gods are vanquished, for by this cancellation the gods never existed. Worse, of course, is implied for the gods are all within *God*; whether as a pantheistic spirit of harmony through the cosmos, an abstract ideal or a physical body in Heaven, God is placed outside this play. By the cancelling effect these two speeches have upon each other the gods, and finally God, (though of course not named) are negated and become nothing.

At the end of the Renaissance, as religious strife and a distaste for the old hopeful spirit of humanism mingled with the coming age of astronomical questioning and objective science, an immense pessimism invades the European mind alongside its brighter spirit of inquiry and interest. *Lear* is a modern play because it leaves the Renaissance behind and looks towards a future that decentres God by placing man at the centre of the world and then decentres man by showing that the earth revolves around man at once the hero and centre of the universe and, yet, an insignificant part of the universe he contemplates. The two exist uneasily side by side gnawing at each other. *Lear* is the crisis of the early stages of this movement; a movement in which a notion of a universal, non-subjective rationally comprehensible idea of God enters its death throes. Descartes writing in the 1640s puts man at the centre of the universe and by so doing puts at risk all notions of God while trying to prove His very existence. Copernicus, Galileo and Kepler put all notions of man at risk by removing him to an inconsequential corner of the universe.

It is not surprising given the preceding remarks that Act I: scene iv should begin with questioning of what is man. First Lear asks Kent, to which Kent replies simply 'a man Sir' (I.iv.10) and then Lear asks Oswald 'who am I' (I.iv.78) to get the reply 'my lady's Father' (I.iv.79). 'Man's life is' not only 'as cheap as beasts' (II.iv.265), but 'in this little world of man' (III.i.10), reduced to seek answers in himself to questions he puts to himself, man becomes mad. When Lear pronounces judgement on mankind it is by using Edgar disguised as 'Poor Tom' that he does so: 'unaccommodated man is no more but such a poor, bare forked animal as thou art' (III.iv.104–5) he says. But Tom is Edgar in disguise. As 'Tom' man is mad, pitiable, a naked wretch; as Edgar he is noble heroic determined, compassionate. The two sides combine in the image and yet as Tom 'Edgar I nothing am' (II.iii.21). Tom replaces Edgar as man goes mad questioning his own being.

After these two questions the Fool enters. It has often been pointed out that the Fool is far from being either comic or foolish. He begins immediately to point up the reversal of roles involved in the relationship of the Fool to Lear now Lear has ceased to be the king:

> There take my coxcomb.... Why, this fellow has banished two on's daughters, and did the third a blessing against his will: if thou [to Kent] follow him thou must needs wear my coxcomb. (I.iv.99–103)

The Fool then recites a list of proverbial sayings all of which are full of common sense, starting 'have more than thou showest'

(I.iv.116) and finishes it with the riddling 'and keep in-a-door/And thou shalt have more/Than two tens to a score' (I.iv.125). Kent answers 'this is nothing' to the Fool's advice (I.iv.126). To which the Fool replies that nothing was given for the advice (I.iv.128). The Fool turns to Lear and asks him 'can you make no use of nothing, nuncle?' (I.iv.128–9) Lear replies 'nothing can be made out of nothing' (I.iv.130). Both Kent and Lear ignore the Fool's 'truth' which the Fool disguises in rhymes and riddles. Again, we find the social deviant at the centre of a world turned upside down. From which it follows that Lear as king may learn from a fool. 'Teach me' he tells the Fool, who responds by accusing Lear of being the true fool:

> *Lear*: 'Dost thou call me fool, boy?
> *Fool*: All thy other titles thou hast given away...
> *Kent*: This is not altogether fool, my lord. (I.iv.145–7)

Through the Fool, Lear is shown to be the foolish one. The Fool recognises the reversal of roles and plays upon it, not merely accusing Lear of being a fool but also of making his 'daughters [his] mothers' (I.iv.169) and in so doing playing 'bo-beep' (I.iv.173) or a game of hiding like a foolish child. Equally, he accuses Lear of giving away all 'the substance'. The simile which he uses is of cutting the egg in two and leaving himself 'nothing i'the middle'. (I.iv.157) The Fool then presents Lear with another simile:

> *Fool*: Thou wast a pretty fellow...now thou art an O without a figure. (I.iv.188–190)

Through the deception of the physical senses the Fool turns attention to the deception of the rational senses: senses of the mind. In the Fool's eyes Lear becomes the ultimate zero, a nought, or as the Fool says, 'thou art nothing' (I.iv.191). More-over, O is the letter without a figure or a body. Indeed, O is therefore the letter that *is* itself nothing and represents nothing. Lear becomes the letter with nothing in it just as Edmund's letter had nothing in it.[5] Hence, the thing that *can* tell Lear if he exists is the nothingness of his 'shadow':

Lear:　　Who is it that can tell me who I am?
Fool:　　Lear's shadow. (I.iv.227–8)

The Fool as Lear's antithetical nothingness (or shadow) changes places with Lear until Lear emerges as both the Fool and the shadow not merely of himself but of his Fool. As Lear becomes his own fool madness looms up. For the Fool represents the non-rational elements contained in proverbs, riddles, paradoxes and ironies, and yet still remains a repository for sense—a non-sense unrecognised by the undeviated world: the world of Kent and the old-style Lear before he divided his kingdom. Now, having passed through the looking glass into the mirror world of the Fool, Lear finds not the intelligence of non-rational non-sense but finds instead pure nonsense leading to madness. Thus Lear tells of the time 'when nature, being oppress'd, commands the mind to suffer with the body' and of 'this tempest in my mind' (III.iv.13). Robbed of the reality of the social order he is meant to command Lear forfeits his head (the unfigured '0') and empties his mind (the image of the egg) until nothing remains. In the world of the Fool Lear loses his identity as a substance and takes on his role as shadow and ghost. The Fool bridges the gap between these two worlds and therefore his role is ambiguous, hovering between being at once himself and, by being in the shadow of Lear, also a representative of the transitional state of mind in the old king. As the insubstantial creature he is, he vanishes when Cordelia returns to the stage, to be dismissed in an off-stage death.

Alongside the Fool Edgar appears as Tom. I have already argued that Tom embodies both sides of the crisis concerning rationality and objectivity at the time. At one moment the natural philosophers were finding objective facts, the bedrock of future advances toward a rationally adjusted Truth in which time and space, not man, were the measure of the universe. And in the same moment the whole process whereby this was possible was being questioned. Descartes' 'cogito' thinking itself and comprehending its own processes could as needs be rational as mad. Man's new interest in science made him capable of standing aside; a cool detached observer of cold 'factual' evidence independent of his senses. Philosophy, nevertheless, placed men at the centre in a subjective struggle with cognitive and intuitive understanding. It is no coincidence that Descartes, like Tom, fears he is led astray by a devil and at one point Lear calls Tom a 'philosopher' (III.iv.151). Indeed, it is the devil and male sexuality that dominate Tom's philosophy—fear of madness becomes madness itself, a madness which allows repressed sexual urges to rise to the surface dressed up as the promptings of a personal devil.

If the Fool represents another order of sense the madman Tom represents the inner fears and urges of the subconscious. Hence, in the Fool and the madman, non-sense and the non-rational combine to confront the normal social order, reverse it, and in so doing become the norms of behaviour. In this world the Fool and the madman command absolute sense; the world being that of the deviant. Deviation, the rule of the *outcast*, becomes the norm until the end of the play. In this mirror world, that normally would be a negation of the real world, negation becomes positive.

And, yet, in all this a certain intolerance has set in. In the world of the play, before Lear's abdication the Fool and the madman would have been tolerated within the social order as figures of amusement. Now, as the world splits into that of the mores of the outcasts against the social mores of the new political manderins Goneril and Regan, the new order *cannot* tolerate either the Fool or madman for they are now a *challenge* to the *new order* on behalf of the *old*. In this sense Gloucester's, Kent's and Lear's bewailing an age gone by, a social order passed, is apposite both to the political world of the play and to the historical milieu of its writing. As the new order accedes to power it makes the old order become as nothing, as never having existed. Ideologically it seeks to make the old order vanish away—a simple negative. However, in *Lear* the reversal makes the legitimate power (that of Regan and Goneril) the usurpers while making Lear (who *willingly* abdicates) a rebel. A rebel thus faces two usurpers. Legitimacy has been turned upside down. Hence, Lear as a legitimate-rebel represents not a mere negative but a positive antithesis to the ruling power: a negation of that power. Yet, Lear has given over power to his daughters. Thus, while they appear as usurpers, they are, in fact, entitled to their power. These sisters represent a power that is held by people who do not command the law. Hence, they are rebels. However, this negative aspect is opposed by the fact that they rule by the king's consent. This is why Lear and his daughters must die, for, in their

73

juxtapositions (Lear as king-not-king and rebel, the sisters as queens-not-queens and rebels) they cancel each other out leaving open the possibility, indeed the necessity, of a new order to follow. As they negate each other they create a vacuum which sucks in the invaders from France, reduces law to the mock trial of the absent sisters by Lear, Tom and the Fool and leads to the revolt of Cornwall's servants against the unnatural cruelty of plucking out Gloucester's eyes. Indeed, as Gloucester says, summing up the world situation of the play 'tis the times' plague, when madmen lead the blind' (IV.i.46).

At the beginning of this chapter I posed the idea of the 'never-to-be-articulated dialogue' or now to define it more closely, of the 'never-said'. Throughout this essay I have tried to define the area in which this operates via deviation, mirroring and negation. I mentioned that much of this 'not said' in *King Lear* is tied to the definition of the sexes and sexuality in the play. I shall now return to that problem.

Man has three roles in this play all of them in consequence of women's roles. The three male types are the *child*, the *impotent* and the *pregnant* man. The first of these ties up closely with the inabilities of old age and the concept of reversal that I've discussed. Goneril says of her father 'old fools are babes again' (I.iii.20) and Lear speaking of Cordelia makes the ambiguous statement, (ambiguous because reversible), about setting his rest 'on her kind nursery' (I.i.123).

The impotent man is tied closely to the senile and the child. This manifests most obviously in regard to the act of blinding whereby man is made dependent and useless. It closely ties in with madness. Kent prophesies 'Be Kent unmannerly when Lear is mad' (I.i.144–5).

It is Goneril and Regan who usurp their husbands' places. It is they who wield power. Thus as 'unnatural hags' (II.iv.276) they refuse to act their allotted roles and masculinise themselves. Goneril talking to Edmund says 'I must change arms at home, and give the distaff/into my husband's hands' (IV.ii.17–18). In so doing she gives Albany back his penis via the female 'penis': the tongue. Frequently the men in the play attack the voracious sensual and sexual appetite of these masculine-women, Eves that have usurped Adam. The word 'monster' (III.v.100) is associated with them, especially with the idea of breeding; the new woman is a monster whose sexual appetite is fed but not satiated by man. Lear says of them:

> The fitchew nor the soiled horse goes to't
> With a more riotous appetite.
> Down from the waist they are Centaurs,
> Though women all above. (IV.vi.121-4)

The sisters make of themselves 'masculine' centaurs desexing themselves. The female function of birth is therefore discarded by these women. Regan's 'full flowing stomach' (V.iii.75) contains anger as vomit: the child of monstrous birth, for Lear has cursed them to sterility. In cursing women's fertility Lear curses man's own potency. Indeed, Lear exclaiming, 'all germens spill at once that make ingrateful man' makes this clear (III.ii.8-9). Moreover, this reversal of roles attacks not only sexuality but *textuality*—the very 'grammar' and order of the *cosmic text*. Alanus de Insulis tells us, 'the sex of active genus trembles shamefully at the way in which it degenerates into passivity. Man is made woman... the craft of magic Venus hermaphrodites him. He is both predicate and subject, he becomes likewise of two divisions, he pushes the laws of grammar too far'.[6] And 'Hic Mulier' pronounced in 1620:

> Since the daies of *Adam* women were never so masculine. Masculine in their genders and whole generations, from Mother, to the youngest daughter; Masculine in Numbers from one to multitudes, Masculine in Case...Masculine in Mood, from bold speech, to impudent action; and Masculine in Tense....most monstrous.[7]

But I would contend this goes further. Lear, we have seen is represented by the Fool in the letter 'O'. At one point Albany says of the deeds of his wife, 'most monstrous! O!' (V.iii.159). How do these tie together? I would contend that this second 'O', even though it is obviously an *exclamation*, is also a hieroglyph or graffito representation of the female genitalia. Angela Carter points out that:

> In the stylization of graffiti, the prick is always represented erect, in an attitude of enquiry... it points upward, it asserts. The hole is open, an inert space, like a mouth waiting to be filled.... The male is positive, an exclamation mark. Woman is negative. Between her legs lies nothing but zero, the sign for nothing, that only becomes something when the male principle fills it with meaning.[8]

Thus, the argument would run like this. The female genitalia have been obliquely referred to already as secret, forbidden and evil in the play. Hence, although the following quotations all refer to the room or bed of illicit sex they also refer to the *absolute place* where illicit sex takes its course: the female sexual organs. Edgar talks of 'the dark and vicious place' (V.iii.171) and Regan of the 'forfended place' (V.i.11). We have already had references to woman's voracious sexuality. It is this greed to possess a man as a sexual object, the desire of both women for Edmund, that initiates the final action. No wonder women's sexual organs are a monstrous 'O' and an exclamation of nothingness. But this exclamation would also be an insult. Hence, the place of breeding, of conception (and 'knowledge'), in the vocabulary of the play is made equivalent with nothingness and blasphemy which in turn is linked to the feminine and hence to Lear. The place of women's role, that of breeding, has been forfeited; that role has been taken up by men.

Numerous examples of this redirection of sexual function can be found in the play. Kent says, 'I cannot conceive' (I.i.11), Gloucester asks 'My son Edgar. Had he a hand to write this? A heart and brain to breed it in?' (I.ii.54–5) Lear says, 'thou but rememberest me of mine own conception' (I.iv.65), and Edmund says to Edgar, 'the profits of my death were very pregnant' (II.i.74–5) as Goneril says to Edmund, 'conceive and fare thee well' (IV.ii.25). Edgar, is 'pregnant to good pity' (IV.vi.220) and Regan says of Oswald, 'our sister's man is certainly miscarried' (V.i.5).

Lisa Jardine points out a further twist:

> Curiously, Shakespeare appears to support this inversion theme in *King Lear* when he has Lear succumb to 'a fit of the mother'—hysteria, a rising up of the womb out of its

place—quite inappropriately for a man: 'O! how this mother swells up toward my heart!/*Hysterica passio*—down, thou climbing sorrow,/Thy element's below' (II.iv.54–6). Lear, subjected to the misrule of his domineering and scolding daughters, responds with a peculiarly female malady: The womb is frequently subject to suffocation. Suffocation is the name doctors give to a constriction of the vital breathing caused by a defect in the womb. This hinders the woman's breathing. It happens whenever the womb moves from its proper place. [It was believed in antiquity and down to the sixteenth century that the womb could move about the body, lodge in the throat, and cause choking.] Then, as a result of a chill in the heart, women sometimes swoon, feel a weakness in the heart, or suffer dizziness.[9]

Now, all these usages refer primarily to understanding and to intellectual conception, the ability to conceive a plan or idea. Equally, they are all references to the birth process. The point is that as man is feminised so is he made impotent by becoming a monstrous 'O'. Endowed with a womb man nevertheless is unable to give birth to understanding. Man's birth function is tied to illusion, lies and madness. Even Edgar's 'pity' is born too late to change the action of the play. By changing the birth-giving role of women for the power of men, women forfeit their wombs to men whom they have destroyed in so doing. Man cannot 'conceive' in this play and no male character is able to conceive or understand the whole of the tragic situation. Man's conception leads ultimately to intellectual miscarriage.

And so what of the answer to the riddle I posed of the unspoken? 'Truth' is blocked through this inability to conceive one avenue to meaning. That way nothing *lies* (an admirable pun?). The womb-endowed-man is a man born of disharmony. The unarticulated is also bound up with 'silence'. At key points in the play the truth is not spoken: Cordelia 'cannot heave her heart into [her] mouth' (I.i.90–1); France talks of the 'history unspoke' (I.i.235); The Fool keeps 'mum' (I.iv.194); Kent's plain speaking is taken for sophistry by Cornwall; Gloucester pitying Lear says, 'no words, no words, hush' (III.vi.178); Edgar's pitying tears almost but not quite betray his silence. Silence conceals the

'Truth' and thereby conspires by consent with the negation and nothingness that is embodied paradoxically in the action. Thus, the riddle is answered, if it ever will be—that the play's meaning is itself contained in an abysmal silence. And therein lies the grand paradox of the play. The harmony of man and cosmos present before the play begins is often regretted but never articulated (Gloucester talks only of the *present* squabbles). Hence, harmony becomes an unarticulated positive presence outside the play or to be precise and paradoxical a positive absence *in* the play. Disharmony is the presence of negation within the play but because it *is* present and does animate the action it becomes peculiarly *positive*. As harmony is absent, in the terms of the play harmony's absence becomes peculiarly negative. For the world the play creates, harmony is meaning: to *act* harmoniously would restore meaning to that world. Harmony is the play's lost origin (does this have something to do with the absence of *mothers*?). But, the world of the play is disharmonious: an anti-truth.

Hence, a complex paradox sets in. By being absent truth cannot be uttered in the play, untruth can be uttered and frequently is: *hence, untruth as lies gains meaning*. Truth cannot have a relationship with itself: it is indivisible. Untruth can have a relationship. Only through relationships can meaning appear: one thing against another, compared to another. But these relationships are set up through lies. They, nevertheless, are not false. Does this mean the relationships in the play are 'true' and in what sense? Language *is* communication but silence veils the truth and stops its articulation. Can that which is *not said* be true in an art form that almost exclusively relies on words? Can truth have significance where it is *not* present and, yet, can untruth have presence where it is present and, yet, present as nothing? These are questions that go beyond literary criticism and limit it. So, now, 'I know the riddle' (V.i.38) as Goneril says 'no more the text is foolish' (IV.ii.37). And, yet, does not the text answer the riddle with something like this paradoxical sentence:

The sentence that is true is also lying.
'Is this the promised end?' (V.iii.263)—Perhaps.

George Steiner writes with a complacent certitude that, 'Shakespeare could play the speculative instincts of Baconian empiricism against the archaic authority of a daemonic world. His assent to the supernatural is, therefore, tentative—and the richness of the dramatic treatment springs from incertitude.'[10]

What I have tried to show in this study of *Lear* is not a certain manipulative authority in this work of Shakespeare but the charting of a deeply rooted anxiousness both in the play and in the age. Shakespeare's adherance to the supernatural in this play is not that of an involvement with externals but with, as Steiner says ironically, 'daemonism', a 'daemonism' rooted in the self and its relationship to external forces. It is precisely between Baconian empiricism and archaic animism or, as I argue, between the horns of Copernican theory and Descartianism that this anxiousness is located: a fear about the relationship of self to a world of 'meanings'.

6

Reading and Death

Considering Detective Fiction in the Nineteenth Century

The nineteenth-century detective story forms a bridge between late romanticism and emerging modern literature. Late romanticism was preoccupied with the cult of personality, with the motives and psychology of that personality, with rampant and eccentric individualism and with an organic theology. Detective fiction, however much it later recuperated the romanticism from which it emerged, joins romanticism to an emergent modernism which felt itself freed, from the necessities of a theological and organic unity, freed also from a theological moral purpose (in as much as detective fiction is 'outside' real life and therefore fantastic) and freed from the cult of personality (in as much as personality for the nineteenth-century moderns becomes synonymous with art and art a synonym for abstract thought). The modernist self is that self abstracted from itself (defined within art for art's sake) absorbed in watching its own processes of creation. Self-consciousness links late romanticism and early modernism. As such the detective story forms a very special link in the emergence of the full theoretically based modernism of the early years of the twentieth century, for Edgar Allan Poe's theory of the short story is a theorisation of 'modern' in the early avant-garde, and that theory is *de facto* a definition of his detective tales.

But this link is not merely artistic for, paradoxically, the detective story idealises personality as pure thought (abstracts or aetherealises it) and by so doing extinguishes the subject in its discourse. Indeed, here the subject is defined only in relationship to 'thought' and all thought in detective fiction revolves around criminal deviancy (always expelled). Within this paradox ('pure' thought embodied as art-object) the detective story unites movements of fragmentation in the nineteenth century. Neither mere escapism nor peripheral fable, the detective story is the very agent whereby the art of the fictionalist and the analysis of the 'scientist' attempted, however unconsciously, to reconcile the contradictions of a society under the dual pressure of eccentric individualism and dubiously safe conformism. This chapter is an attempt to consider the formal properties of detective fiction and the complex interrelations between detective fiction, reading and death, between murder and creation.

By removing itself from 'real' life and by becoming more abstract, and for the reader more abstracting, the detective story fulfilled a basic aim of early modernism. Its self-absorption abolished subject matter in favour of form. However, it translated that form, telling the reader that it was presented *not* as the finished form in which fiction traditionally appeared but that this form represented a *process* of 'reading'. Hence, the tale is not the tale of the teller but of the reader (reading itself abolished by becoming a form of 'listening' to a narrator-guide). Detective writing in the nineteenth century is therefore a continuing tale of what it means to read: a constant search for meaning among a jumble of signs and signals patterned as if random yet always concentric, a concentricism guided by and organised within the mind of the detective (the eccentric outsider) upon whom the responsibility of organisation and revelation rests (modernism's belief in the organisational abilities of the reader).

This adventurous quest, the fictional representation of what it means to read, places emphasis upon the purchaser of the tale and diverts interest ultimately away from the tale itself. And, yet, who notices this movement? The detective story diverts the reader from himself within the abstraction of reading as amusement and as diversion (but at the cost of a neuroticism and an addiction). As an invocation of the process of reading, these tales, in their innocuous vitality, engage the mind of the reader in order to divert the mind in order to abolish that mind within the pre-ordained fate laid out in the text. This text is rendered irreplaceable (except by other detective tales) and inexorable through the omniscience of an author (himself rendered merely another reader: 'now what shall I make happen next? What would Holmes do in this situation?'). The detective tale thus hails the supremacy of free-will (the mind) and, yet, shackles it to a totalising and inescapable fate.

Within the confines of this dilemma the detective story understands a notion of psychology, but a psychology determined by *consciousness*—the mind considers its own processes through abstract contemplation and hence consciousness becomes a determining factor for the unconscious. Freud's case histories, so like detective tales themselves, bear this out. Thus Freud determines the unconscious processes by knowing the manifestly conscious. The known always defines the unknown in Freud's case studies in order that Freud can invoke the very primacy of the unknown and unknowable unconscious (precisely always known and knowable to the reader-analyst: psychology as irony).

In detective fiction the 'repressed' is already known to the culprit and to the victim and this knowledge is conscious at all times, working as a form of fate, externalised, and represented externally for the subject upon whom it works its power. The power is always acknowledged as such by everybody at all times in the detective story. In the nineteenth-century detective story the culprits leave *clues* because they wish to leave clues, because the fate of the story demands they leave clues—a trail always hot, a narrative therefore always short. Personality is unnecessary when external; its signs function independently. By this personality becomes a series of external narrative moments—the individual culprit is interpretable *in absentia*, being only a projection of these moments. Each moment is consciously manifest, always given, always offered space, never hidden for the reader, never unconscious. The detective story *therefore confronts psychology*, denies it, renders it impotent. As a projection of various signs the victim is re-constructed in the mind of the analyst in order for a final deduction to be made. The deduction concerns the crime *not* the criminal. The criminal then becomes another sign, another clue, rather than a resolution of all clues gathered within his personality. In the classic detective tale the criminal always wishes to be caught. He is the analyst's brother, confrère, co-conspirator, playing bluff on the level of abstract thought. There is a game, a set of rules, a sequence in which personality must be extinguished in order for the rules to work. The rules of the game, of the genre, determine the sequence and the game into which personality fits, a personality defined as independent of the game only in as much as the genre attempts a naturalisation of character (touches of social realism). Like all participant rituals the game of analysis played as detection allows for an annulment of personality, a temporary hiatus of egocentricism in *communal* action.

In becoming a detective, in becoming a culprit, characters acknowledge bonds of brotherhood, bonds of relationship. Any game can by played providing one knows the ritual and the *technique*. Hence the craftsman using this technique abstracts personality while the artist demands it. Characters are consummate technical craftsmen, manipulating the tools of a trade which are the equipment of trained players. The reader follows the moves of the characters as a spectator but a spectator who participates and who knows the rules, who knows, beforehand, the acceptable conclusion. The player sequence requires the analyst to reconstruct an already given trail (the culprit has already been there). The analyst-detective wins if he does so. The culprit does *not* lose, he wins if he escapes or if he is 'caught' (one cannot undo the crime, one cannot 'stop' the game).

There is then no character-analysis in detective fiction that can occur outside of the analytic game. The culprit already knows that the detective knows that the reader knows. Naïveté is abolished in detective fiction as we are all technically adept at the genre—readers as detective as culprits (what would we have done to evade the detective in such and such circumstance?).

It is not personality that is projected in a form of psychology but personality *as a condition of artistic form* that is designated in the detective story. Personality is, as we have said, externalised as a series of clues, of closely related signs. But these signs are simply one of the conditions of the narrative form of this type of fiction—they belong to the genre's code. Thus they relate to the craft of the genre. This relationship is intimate and essential; the sequence of clues is a formal element, a part of the text's design, and, as such, the consequence of, and yet provider of, the text's form. Considered as a series of formal and consequential juxtapositions it is these the analyst weaves into personality, emphasising the crime and not the criminal. Indeed, there are no criminals in classic detective fiction only players, invokers, initiators of the game of analysis while the victim is worthless, un-remarked, a necessary yet inconsequential sacrifice, just another clue—without moral worth. The victim lends no blame to the culprit, the culprit bears no moral culpability. He plays the analytic game.

In the game of 'hare and hounds', the culprit enjoys a position as artist and logician. A pure rationalist, he *calculates* the odds of a crime and the winnings; for he is a technician of death, of death without violence (a violence devoid of malice). Moreover, he kills for killing's sake (*l'art pour l'art*) and he bows to the detective who is, after all, only another reader at this stage (perhaps of a superior kind).

Yet the culprit is extinguished in this acknowledgement of formal mastery. The form envelops him, and his personality becomes art. As exterior signs the clues give 'body' to the narrative and give it a true subject: accumulation of other clues. Thus the crime equals a gross accumulation of 'facts' which neutralises itself when another formal element comes forward. The culprit in the confession unites and abolishes clues and the confession ends by a narrative within a narrative, a final signature to the original deed, the original creative act (I kill, I therefore create). The text generates itself from a creative act, the subject of which (even if theft or blackmail) is always death. The culprit becomes an artist precisely because he kills, killing in order to create his confessed narrative—an artist in search of an *attentive* and *captive* (who is detained, detective or reader?) audience. This is an intimate audience of one, the detective himself as the surrogate reader.

The culprit, *not* the detective, allows for the resolution of the tale. Yet by becoming a principle of unity, a focus for organicism in the text, the culprit, nevertheless, reminds us that he is an-other projection (maybe not the ultimate projection) of a series of clues, of formal signs of a reading and of a *textual* rendering. The clues lead to a perpetrator of a crime as part of that textual rendering of crime as artistic production. The culprit then becomes a formal element of the text, complementing the detective as one of the twin principles of the textual organisation of detective fiction.

Personality as art, art as formal juxtaposition, whence the culprit is the idealisation of individualism (killing others as confirmation of his own existence) at the very moment the individual metamorphoses into a text whose moves must be read and interpreted. As the foremost element of a detective tale (the crime as such is not an element in itself being the accumulation of *all* the other elements both of the culprit and his detective or police pursuers) the culprit becomes part of his crime, so that to find the criminal is *per se* an act of reductive reading for one rather needs to read the 'crime' laid out as tale (which is simply to say one must finish the whole story). The criminal is artist and text. Indeed, he is the very signal to the reader of the literary element in the tale (its grammatical and syntactic originator and symptomatic surface).

Compared to the culprit the figure of the detective only seems more important. But this grandeur of the detective is bought at the expense of his necessity in the tale. Precisely because the culprit is the *author* of the story (author of the crime) he cannot step out of the tale. But it is precisely because the detective is merely a reader that he can *appear* to step out of the tale. The detective appears to operate externally to the text in which he appears. The personality of a reader inhabits him but this does not fill him. Accepted as more than fictional (as real) the detective is a cipher for reading, a medium of readership, a facade for the process of reading a criminal action (here the very text itself).

The criminal/artist forgets himself in his act (murder/the art creation) and extinguishes his personality by putting it *all* in the service of the act. Nevertheless, the act, the murder, the artistic creation embody him and encapsulate, as in amber, a memorial to the murderer/artist's presence. Art is here—the artist was here as murder *is* here so there must be a murderer. Murder/art reconstructs the culprit through a testimonial which acts as the *text's* (the deed's) *memory*. Only temporarily does the act (the murder, the art-object) forget the culprit, for the perpetrator *becomes* the totality of his perpetration and hides within it as its *unconscious*. This the detective searches out—sniffing for the latency he suspects. This detective never forgets himself for as reader he is never 'lost' in creation. He is neither 'caught out' nor lets his guard down.

The classic nineteenth-century detective remembers himself via his concentration on abstraction. Hence, the detective is supremely he-who-thinks rather than he-who-acts (the criminal).

Never initiating the action, the detective plays always the third move (the second is played by *the police* unable to make headway in their inquiries) turning an initial inaction into an eventual passivity which, through its very passivity, becomes an active agent of retribution, recovery and resolution. Every detective is thus Descartes reconstructing a *cogito* in the presence of a diversionary devil whose very diversions (false clues) give eventual access to a preconstructed 'reality' in the tale. Indeed, the very 'falseness' of these red herrings helps to create a 'unified' reality ('why', asks the detective, 'this false clue and not another?' The detective knows the false clues).

The culprit lives in a world of the future (how to both escape *and* meet the detective in a final rendezvous). He is, however, determined by his meeting with the detective, who represents the future of the mounting of the gallows. Meanwhile, the detective suffers from nostalgia, from an endless preoccupation with memory; a memory constrained to follow a determined path back down its own processes and searching for an original moment, a moment of primacy, of the unique and original, of authorship and the birth of the creative act. This *moment of origination* finds itself *in the future* at the meeting with the culprit. The culprit's memory is restored to him through the detective ('this is what it was and how you did it') at the moment the culprit confesses ('I know what it was and how I did it'). The culprit is forgotten only to be remembered. He consciously forgets (refuses to acknowledge) until he knows he must acknowledge his deed.

This is not a case of 'repression' for the criminal is always consciously aware of his act, and his demeanour is a constant and knowing *provocation* to the detective. Hence, the criminal always believes the detective is aware of his presence as culprit. Consequently the culprit flaunts himself in his clues—*leaves his signature* everywhere (a drop of blood, a fingerprint, a footprint). The culprit looks into the eyes of the detective as into a mirror—he confirms his presence. The detective may or may not know who the culprit is but the culprit needs reassurance of his crime (his existence). The detective is flattered by this acknowledgement of his presence, even if he does not know the identification of the culprit (a thing he usually does know). Both participants gain presence via the analytic game, via their postures within it. The problem for the analyst is not to find the criminal (who is always 'on stage' for the playing area is always enclosed: a house, a drawing room where all the participants gather) but 'proving' or working out *how* a crime was committed (the 'locked room'). The culprit acts and thinks to allow the detective to think and act—perfect complementarity of dancing partners in crime. The game is resolved when detective *meets* culprit and both acknowledge the presence of the other (culprit: 'How did you know it was me?' Detective: 'You gave yourself away when...').

In detective fiction there are no 'imperfect' crimes, for all crimes are perfect by their finality (for victim and culprit) but they are also perfect in another way. We have said that the culprit is a craftsman and technician; in these stories moreover, he has to 'get caught' to justify his existence. In so doing the detective (the 'best' brain for the job) accepts a subordinate role and by so doing accedes to the importance of the criminal (although the crime may be minor—at least unimportant).

The perfect crime is therefore precisely the one where the culprit is caught and his ability acknowledged by the 'best' mind for the job ('You nearly had me fooled', says the detective). This 'nearly' is what gratifies the culprit for the machinery of his plot (*the* plot) is almost perfect—it requires to give it perfection the meeting between detective and criminal; *that* makes the crime perfect. At this meeting the detective (an epicure of crime as well as a collector of cases and a connoisseur of criminals) tells the criminal that his craftsmanship, his technique and his *finesse* (his style) have *all* been thoroughly investigated (totally read). The culprit is gratified and ennobled in such company. He stages his whole performance for such a response.

Having given himself away the culprit awaits his reward, which is the hangman's noose upon another stage, while the detective pockets the loot (his wages). 'The wages of sin is death' becomes the ironic motto of this duo, for the detective finds the lost origin (the creative act) was an act of 'bloody murder' and he is paid to do so by another admiring audience (the police) just as the culprit mounts the scaffold to find his own destination in an act of reciprocal murder (his own this time). It is this noose and this death that confirm the criminal's ability, his craft and his function—in death he finds a perfect role and a justified status in society. The great expectations of the culprit end with finding momentary fame (notoriety) and position (social standing). Truly the price he pays gains him a glorious reward.

The law of talion demands 'an eye for an eye' and this the detective story provides, fundamentally the channelling of the 'revenge tragedy' into a new and more vital genre, a genre, more-over, which denies the teachings of a *New Testament* forgiveness in order to reawaken the Jehovian tendencies of an *Old Testament* fundamentalism, precisely based upon adherence to the law, 'repayment' and revenge based upon 'The Book'. All characters in the detective story bear the mark of Cain.

Moreover, this law of talion is enacted upon the body of the culprit just as the body of the victim was acted upon by the criminal. The circle completes itself only if the culprit can externalise his passion and complete self-murder via this detour upon the innocent. The operation of a death drive means that suicide is always accomplished *lawfully* by execution, illegality hence restores legality and returns the law to its proper place. The law, indeed, operates above and beyond its representatives (the police) whose helplessness brings them to the detective's door. In his eccentric and external position the detective becomes the representative of a fundamental law of return, a law which transcends the social law and directs it. In the very act of going-beyond-the-law the detective more fully upholds it.

However, it is the culprit who provokes the law in the first place. It is he, not the detective, who invokes and then awaits the prescription of the law; he becomes its agent and its victim through his confession via the medium of the detective. Having crossed the line representing the limit (the limit is always known, as is the 'beyond' of the limit, when we say we've gone *beyond* it) the culprit recuperates the limit in his excessiveness (his provocation upon the taboo of death and human sacrifice). By going beyond the law both culprit and detective uphold the law in a more sublime way. They operate as new and more sublime re-presentatives of an order which commands that which organises the social. The circle of revenge closes on the scaffold but the victim (the culprit) has now gone beyond the laws governing the social into a dimension governing the world of abstractions (harmony, order, even laws of energy perhaps) a world of universal values and *absolute* relationships; a universe governed by paradox.

The violence of the scaffold (never mentioned until a later development in the genre) restores the imbalance caused by the violence of the murder (also never mentioned—only the victim's *body* is so mentioned: dead meat dissected). The detective, just as the culprit, is rendered unnecessary at the end of the story—they have met and been 'paid off' by the forces of social order. Order is, therefore, restored, although social order is rarely threatened and the detective finds himself without a job and without any more tale within which to exist (he too 'dies' textually).

Culprit, victim and detective all 'die' (as if a tragedy had been enacted) but not so that a new order can take over (so that the *really new* can begin) but so that the forces of conservatism can be restored and refreshed. Society is rendered safe only when the detective also is rendered impotent, his analytic rage spent, (for the detective is obsessive and professionally paranoid). The individual triumphs in his demise, parades his potency in his moment of impotence. Social harmony: social and universal order is restored in laughter ('of course so that's who did it!—I should have known', says the reader). The detective story in the nineteenth century allows the tragic to become melodrama, allowing restoration amid fragmentation, causing the comic to become the 'natural', for the detective story's model is always comic, restorative, restitutive, recuperative, therapeutic—always life as perpetual analytic comedy.

7

Metaphor and Reality, the 'Book', the Cosmos:

Hands of God and man

To explain the universe: a metaphor. The universe of phenomena tells of another universe, coexistent with, yet transcendent of, that universe; a universe that is *the* expression of divinity, that is the gesture of and symbol of a moment outside its history, the moment of a divine logos. And that logos is the representative of a law which marks that logos with its presence and declares itself in the phenomenal cosmos. The pneumatic logos is expressed in the symbolic creation, a creation which points within itself and beyond itself back to that divine logos and back from that to a moment that is a non-moment 'notated' in mysticism as 'silence'. This 'point' of silence, in which the logos falters, is the point from which the logos goes forth into time and into space. The logos marks out a chronology which conceives itself in terms of spatial relationships.

The mystic, the alchemist, the kabbalist, as travellers toward that primal 'silence' fill the void of phenomena with metaphor; things gesture toward a hidden essence and the adept 'reads' each gesture as a point marked in space. Interpretation of objects is conceived in terms of 'reading'. The adept reads the signs of a divine presence ever veiled behind and within and beyond the manifest tokens of a mundane 'language': the language of objects.

As theological exegesis turns into literary criticism so the world turns into a book written by the finger of God. The Law, already existing *with* God, written by a divine hand neither of man nor God, rules a speech sacred to the deity. For the adept, understanding the divine presence through the 'act' of the book, the book becomes the representative of divine presence. The divine presence finds itself in *the* book, and the divine expression filling the forms of the law fills itself again with its creation; a creation which is interpretable according to the formal laws governing the rhetoric of textuality. God, the supreme artist, finds his first 'critics' in the Magi. Indeed, these Magi guarantee their position because to them their innate *critical faculty* manifestly proves the presence of their object (knowledge of God). Thus, they prove the validity of their 'objective' observations by the processes of their subjectivity. A very special tautology begins to operate. The divine 'spark' in man empathises through reading with the divine spark of the divinity. Again tautology, the text that presupposes a latent spoken logos (the spontaneous expression of a divine creative 'word') finds that logos within itself as a *manifest* property of the laws governing textuality.

For the adept, this special textuality, preformed by divine laws, no longer merely describes the spoken word it supposedly hides, is no longer *mere* metaphor. Here, metaphor becomes literal, becomes again tautological. It works with a literal power, describing itself as it does so. Metaphor presupposes a *complex* world to be interpreted, and interpretation presupposes and works within that metaphor.

In his excellent book, *The World and the Book*, Gabriel Josipovici has traced the history of the metaphor of the 'book' from classical times to the Renaissance. From the epigraph that heads the chapter titled 'The World as a Book' Josipovici details the history of this metaphor through such writers as Dante, Origen, St. Augustine and Leonardo da Vinci. Josipovici offers another example from Hugh of St. Victor:

> The notion that God works through history [says Josipovici] was reinforced by the notion that God is the author of a second book, the Book of Nature. Hugh of St. Victor, writing in the twelfth century, put it like this:
> 'For this whole visible world is a book written by the finger of God, that is, created by divine power; and individual creatures are as figures therein not devised by human will but instituted by divine authority to show forth the wisdom of the invisible things of God. But just as some

illiterate man who sees an open book looks at the figures but does not recognise the letters: just so the foolish natural man who does not perceive the things of God sees out-wardly in these visible creatures the appearances but does not inwardly understand the reason. But he who is spiritual and can judge all things, while he considers outwardly the beauty of the work inwardly conceives how marvellous is the wisdom of the Creator'.[1]

This 'book' made itself available only to those who could see, who had clear insight. As Josipovici points out, such an inner language written by divine hand opens to allow an 'accurate depiction of reality', a reality hidden and yet an 'open book', latent and yet manifest.[2]

To one religion, says Josipovici, this metaphor took on a dramatically literal and urgent meaning—to Christianity. Through the text of the Bible that 'moment' out of existence reaches into history and opens a space for itself. Of Christianity, he writes that, 'never has there been such faith in the phenomenal. What guarantees this faith is the Incarnation, for it is the eruption into time of the eternal, into space of the infinite'.[3] The world of appearance and of visibility is guaranteed by the presence of the invisible, outside history, acting as its law and as the form of its fiction. A symbol guarantees narrative, for to the Christian, 'Christianity is unique among the major religions in that it depends entirely on the historical fact of the Incarnation'.[4]

For the medieval Christian world-mythologiser this has important repercussions. Of Dante's *Divine Comedy*, we are told:

The poem reminds us that it starts on Good Friday and ends on Easter Sunday, and that Dante's descent into Hell and his ascent to Heaven exactly parallel Christ's Passion and Resurrection. So that, just as the Christian who partakes of the eucharist re-enacts in himself Christ's redemptive action, so the reader of the poem re-enacts Dante's journey, which is itself an analogue to the eucharistic action... Dante's allegory signifies what it does, not because *Dante* means it to, but because *God* does. For

Dante history, if rightly apprehended, yields a pattern which points to God's work.[5]

Yet this metaphor is far older than Christianity and belongs both to the pagan world of the Greeks as to the Hebraic world of the Talmud and Torah and the traditions of those Jews, who 're-discovered' the metaphor through Kabbalism (the study of *tradition* by occult means). In this they were concerned with a certain type of order; an order, and a harmony, that was made manifest via the vitality of a divine language—Hebrew; a language whose origins were supernatural, the natural language of the deity, a language within which the world gave itself over to human understanding and which had power of creation (through its syntactic combinations) in the world. The letter becomes supreme in reminding man of his relationship with and correspondence to the divinity. It acts as the emblem of a world memory:

> This efficacy of the study of the Torah is derived from its correspondence with the world. The Torah is conceived by the Zohar as the 'blueprint' wherewith God provided Himself for the creation. 'When God resolved to create the world, He looked into the Torah, into its every creative word, and fashioned the world accordingly: for all the worlds and all the actions of the worlds are contained in the Torah' every word presenting a symbol, every jot and tittle concealing a mystery.
>
> The study of the Torah and the endeavour to discover its hidden meanings thus becomes one of the foremost duties of a son of Israel. 'For he who concentrates his mind on the Torah and penetrates into its inner mysteries sustains the world'. On the other hand, 'he who neglects the study of the Torah is as if he destroyed the world'.
>
> Parallel with the correspondence which exists between the Torah itself and the world is the correspondence between the precepts of the Torah and the component parts of the human body.[6]

Again Josipovici:

Such an attitude takes it for granted that there is an analogy between man and God. Not only is man made in God's image; in some sense, God is *in* man....

The universe, then, is a structure of relations, created by God and perceivable by man in his mind's eye. It is non-organic, quantitative, something that is made by an artificer rather than planted by a gardener. But if this is so then it is possible for the artifacts of man to be made according to the same principles, thus providing not an imitation of a fragment of the visible universe, but a model or analogue of the universe itself.[7]

Through his reading of God's text Man is reminded of God as an external force and of the Godhead within himself. Man imitates God as a repetition in the finite (to misquote Coleridge) of divine authorship. Edgar Allan Poe as a late magi, writing in *Eureka* tells us:

The pleasure which we derive from any display of human ingenuity is in the ratio of *the approach* to this species of reciprocity. In the construction of *plot...* fictitious literature, we should aim at so arranging the incidents that we should not be able to determine, of any one of them, whether it depends from any one other or upholds it. In this sense... *perfection* of *plot* is... unattainable—but only because it is a finite intelligence that constructs. The plots of God are perfect. The Universe is a plot of God. [And moreover] that Man, for example, ceasing imperceptibly to feel himself Man, will at length attain that awfully triumphant epoch when he shall recognise his existence as that of Jehovah.[8]

Subjective experience guarantees the objective world. Jewish Kabbalists influence Christian alchemists. Frances Yates writes of the alchemists that, 'the common basis would be a common Christianity, interpreted mystically, and a philosophy of Nature which sought the Divine meaning of the hieroglyphic characters written by God in the universe, and interpreted macrocosm and microcosm through mathematical-magical systems of universal harmony'.[9]

Man is reminded of God while the world and the cosmos

become tablets engraved with the memory of the initial moment. Moreover, man reminded of his divine nature finds his own memory as a text and in a text. Frances A. Yates, quoting an ancient book on memory writes, by way of paraphrase:

> The art of memory is like an inner writing. Those who know the letters of the alphabet can write down what is dictated to them and read out what they have written. Likewise those who have learned mnemonics can set in places what they have heard and deliver it from memory. 'For the places were very much like wax tablets or papyrus, the image like the letters, the arrangement and disposition of the images like the script, and the delivery is like the reading'.[10]

Another thousand years and this ancient alchemic formula for memory is 'rediscovered' by Freud in the metaphor of a 'mystical writing pad', finding the divine, not externally but as an invisible structure within the psyche. Jacques Derrida, the foremost critical analyst of logos, of the mark of 'divine' language and of the imprint of the theology of textuality, has explored and questioned this metaphor. He asks a simple question with profound implications. Can a writing apparatus adequately represent the psyche? If so, how is the psyche produced by and productive of language? How does the psyche signify through a metaphor of writing? Derrida writes of this decisive question:

> We shall let our reading be guided by this metaphoric investment. It will eventually invade the entirety of the psyche. Psychical *content* will be *represented* by a text whose essence is irreducibly graphic. The structure of the physical *apparatus* will be *represented* by a writing machine. What questions will these representations impose upon us? We shall not have to ask if a writing apparatus—for example, the one described in the 'Notes Upon the Mystic Writing Pad'—is a *good* metaphor for representing the working of the psyche, but rather what apparatus we must create in order to represent psychical writing; and we shall have to ask what the imitation, projected and liberated in a machine of something like psychical writing might mean. And not if

the psyche is indeed a kind of text but: what is a text, and what must the psyche be if it can be represented by a text? For if there is neither machine nor text without psychical origin, there is no domain of the psyche without text. Finally, what must be the relationship between psyche, writing, and spacing for such a metaphoric transition to be possible, not only, nor primarily, within theoretical discourse, but within the history of psyche, text, and technology?[11]

Before considering the implications of Derrida's questioning of Freudian metaphor in its relationship to representation and writing, we must turn to Freud's own description of the mystic writing pad:

The Mystic Pad is a slab of dark brown resin or wax with a paper edging; over the slab is laid a thin transparent sheet, the top end of which is firmly secured to the slab while its bottom end rests upon it without being fixed to it. This transparent sheet is the more interesting part of the little device. It itself consists of two layers which cannot be detached from each other except at their two ends. The upper layer is a transparent piece of celluloid; the lower layer is made of thin translucent waxed paper. When the apparatus is not in use, the lower surface of the waxed paper adheres lightly to the upper surface of the wax slab.

To make use of the Mystic Pad, one writes upon the celluloid portion of the covering-sheet which rests upon the wax slab. For this purpose no pencil or chalk is necessary, since the writing does not depend on material being deposited upon the receptive surface. It is a return to the ancient method of writing upon tablets of clay or wax: a pointed stylus scratches the surface, the depressions upon which constitute the 'writing'. In the case of the Mystic Pad this scratching is not effected directly, but through the medium of the covering-sheet. At the points which the stylus touches, it presses the lower surface of the waxed paper on to the wax slab, and the grooves are visible as dark writing upon the otherwise smooth whitish-grey surface of celluloid. If one wishes to destroy what has been written, all that is necessary is to raise the double covering-sheet from the wax slab by a light pull, starting from the free lower end. The close contact between the waxed paper and the wax slab at the places which have been scratched (upon which the visibility of the writing depended) is thus brought to an end and it does not recur when the two surfaces come together once more. The Mystic Pad is now clear of writing and ready to receive fresh inscriptions.[12]

The system of top sheet and protected waxed lower pad represents for Freud the system of perception and the sytem of the repressed unconscious. When the top and bottom sheet (protecting the wax pad) are brought into contact and the stylus applied, a form of writing akin in its process to the depositing of information in the psyche is produced.

Freud's toy machine has four possible movements. In the first, contact is made between the sheets and the applied stylus. At that moment, the latent (or bottom layer) is brought out *through* the manifest layer and both exhibit their interdependence. In the second move the top sheet is withdrawn, thus destroying the manifest layer; no writing is perceptible. On closer examination the wax exhibits the stylus marks but the third position, although it contains the stylus marks in the wax, leaves them *unobtainable*, viewed as they need to be through the top sheet. Hence, the area of the latent is left only as a potential. In the fourth move, the recontacting of the top and bottom sheets, the wax inscription is partially obliterated by the new inscriptions of a new latent level and a new manifest level. The writing pad therefore retains a partial history, but one impossible to regain. In the end history is continually disconnected from its presence in the manifest level and is therefore continually lost.

Initially, the metaphor of the wax pad seems adequate for the representation of the psyche. Derrida comments:

Let us note that the *depth* of the Mystic Pad is simultaneously a depth without bottom, an infinite allusion, and a perfectly superficial exteriority: a stratification of surfaces each of whose relation to itself, each of whose interior, is but the implication of another similarly exposed surface. It joins the two empirical certainties by which we are constituted:

infinite depth in the implication of meaning, in the unlimited
envelopment of the present, and, simultaneously, the
pellicular essence of being, the absolute absence of any
foundation.[13]

The pad fulfils these criteria but, while Freud presents us with
the empirical data of the *permanence* of the impression in the
wax, it is a small problem to disprove the assumption on practical
grounds: once full, the wax as it is re-inscribed will begin to *erase*
former marks. This destroys the analogy with the unconscious
repressed which retains *every* mark, often 'several times' over as
memory traces which *can* be reconstituted through the manifest
level in the act of transference. We are brought back to the idea
that although the manifest level is *manipulated by* the individual
and perceptible to him, it is nevertheless, *paradoxically* beyond
his control, opening him to the analyst via his manifest symptoms, produced by, and productive of, the original repressed idea.
Moreover, the 'machine' wax pad does not run by itself, it
must be manipulated by *outside* hands (theology begins) and thus
it becomes a 'tool'.[14] The pad opens out in its manipulation to
provide the missing referent: the 'other' is always silently present
as observer, witness, manipulator *within* the tool itself as an
inscriber of 'traces'. But, to be a complete model of the psyche,
the wax pad should work by itself, and this it cannot do. 'It is
true too', says Freud 'that once the writing has been erased, the
Mystic Pad cannot "reproduce" it from within'.[15] As an 'auxillary
apparatus' as Freud calls it, the pad is a 'poor' analogy for the
mind.[16]
As the world becomes a text, and as that divine text moves
inward, becoming the guarantor of subjectivity, another
alchemist arises taking his cue both from mystical gnosticism and
psychoanalysis. R.D. Laing, in *The Voice of Experience* comments
that, 'if my own experience is to be believed, in my [Laing's]
adult life I have recalled and re-enacted...experiences long
before birth...before incarnation...scientific reason does not
accept these terms'.[17]
For Laing, science gives way to a mystic analysis of a
remembered experience 'long before birth'; before the intervention of a personal history, the individual takes his divine
imprint, his expressive pneuma from outside history projected

into the space of territorial existence. Having moved into the sphere of the personal, the efficacy of a metaphor becomes literal and makes itself felt. From outside history, history moves recalled from its preformed encapsulation in the laws of a divine predictability—read back through symbolic gesture and the 'signature' of an invisible hand marking the pneuma. The history of the individual and the universe as well as the silent history of history is expressed.

8

Secrets, the Logos and Silence

The Gospel according to St. John

The most banal, and yet most curious, fact about *fictional* literature is that it bears no single and direct relationship to that of which it speaks. That is, within the act of *telling* the text delivers other, sometimes contradictory, messages. Direct statement, incorporating lucidity and clarity, in which that-which-is-spoken-of bears a direct relationship with that-which-speaks is eschewed by the literary in favour of ambiguity, convolution, equivocation and circumlocution. Even the most 'direct' lyrical poem is under the massive constraint, amounting to a law, to act with neither lucidity nor clarity. Ambiguity, convolution, equivocation and circumlocution, the antithesis of that which is contained in one of the most direct needs of language (clear communication between addressor and addressed) are the properties of language's greatest triumph: the literary. Indeed, the fictionally literary incorporates that other need of language: the need to speak in order *to hide a secret*.

Thus, it might be argued that the nature of the fictionally literary is not to communicate but in its complex way to hide communication or to radically delay its ever reaching a destination.

In this, such literature would be concerned with hiding the lucidity of its meaning in a web of delaying clauses. But what would such a meaning be like should one cut through these delays? Of what would such a meaning consist, being itself the product of a syntax dedicated to withholding its presence? In itself the literary would then act to place meaning under a taboo leading the reader away from that 'core' of 'sacred' and yet 'fearful' reality in order to safeguard its existence. The literary would, therefore, perpetuate itself around 'something' that actually denied the presuppositions of the literary as I have outlined it. 'Meaning', removed as the essential element of the literary, is not itself literary.

Literature, encoded as a language of the-secrets-of-the-undisclosed, conditions a response by its refusal to speak. Nevertheless, there is another coding in which the secret is revealed as secret, unravelled as the language that protects it. A text that uses the literary but declares its very redundancy in the face of an absolute 'core' of meaningfulness should be one that tears its own veils and that points to its own futility as literature; futile because totally redundant in the presence of that which it speaks: Truth. Here, then, would be a text that denies its protective custody, that absents itself in the presence of naked meaning.

The Gospel according to St. John deals with the presence of a divine creative Word, a pre-literary, pre-textual Word made present via a text in the world of men. *The Gospel* is a myth not only of creation but of creative power, the creative power of a divine mystery wrapped in divine law and divine Word; a secret that reveals itself by being *in* all things, hidden and yet exposed by being hidden.[1]

However, while we may recognise the devices of literature in this work, the use of a prologue, a narrative, a climax, a denouement, the presence of rhetorical and syntactic devices common to all fiction, we must realise that these tell us nothing, or almost nothing about the mystery of the work if approached in a formalistic way. As I shall hope to show, the form is the content and the content is the form, an inseparable union at whose centre and transcendent of that centre is a silence that prefigures and directs all that can be said of this work. For the peculiarity of this work is its desire to speak of Truth, and the clarity of that Truth; to connect with a transcendent meaning via its transmitter and transmuter, Christ.[2] Its language appears to be concerned with the literal, with a speech of the literal, not with mystery, secrecy or silence.

Nevertheless, in the first instance I do want to approach the text as just that, as pure text, a written work which claims a status beyond other texts; that status being its pre-eminent, pre-figuring and divine position. To look at this work at all is to face immense problems, not only of religious loyalty but of cultural background. Of all Western texts the Bible stands as the supreme end result and as the prefiguring beginning. The end of a tradition in literature, the *King James Bible* prefigures English literature to come. *The Gospel according to St. John* is the mystical, theoretical and theological centre and justification for that very literature, that self-conscious literariness. While a purely literary analysis fails to grasp the creative thrust of *The Gospel*, biblical exegesis ignores the properties of the *literary* language from which its concerns are generated. Thus, both miss vital areas of interest; the former about the creative moment, its incarnation and its embodiment of meaning; the latter the vehicle of that whole previous process.

Literary analysis, however, owes its origins, in part, to theological concerns, the exegesis of God's Word and its unfolding though critical interpretation. A circle is created in which the creative Word unravels its possibilities through the act of elucidation. Thus, the Word unfolds historically from the literal toward the moral and symbolic and reunites with itself on the level of the divine. Temporal elucidation of the Word (via words) returns to the Word its non-historical origin, its 'otherness' even as it acts within temporality. Elucidation, via exegesis, talks 'of' that which ever escapes it: God's Word. Thus, understanding itself it determines a mysterious origin that cannot be understood. The lucidity of language is both reinforced and challenged by God's *clear* 'message'. This Word of God directs elucidation and precedes exegesis, creating the exegetical texts that will talk 'of' it. Hence, this divine language precedes interpretation and creates interpretation while remaining powerful and inexplicable.

This problem is circular and entrapping and it encircles the triple concerns of Word, law and transcendence. It is upon these that I shall concentrate. And, yet, if we pursue the Word we find ourselves constantly in the presence of a blocking device made to delay the revelation of that Word through divine ambiguity and convolution.

I am suggesting that contrary to our expectations *The Gospel according to St. John* incorporates the very delaying devices which we should not expect to find in a text of this sort; a text that purports to deal in clarity, a direct relationship to Truth and a text that declares its language is attempting, in describing miracles and signs, to be describing the literal and not the symbolic or mystical, dealing, as it does, in the *signs of what is* (directly opening doors on to reality).

It is surprising then to find that all this is transmitted via a language dedicated to obscurity and complexity, in which witnesses talk in riddles as much as witness them. For it is the riddle that stands at the heart of *The Gospel* as its ultimate conveyor of meaning. A device as ancient as the riddle, revealer, obscurer and 'perverter' of meaning stands before literature as the first play upon fiction; a knowing understanding of the ambiguity of language in a form of cunning which displays things in a new light and a new way. The riddle bends meaning, refracts and conditions and astonishes explication by playing with a reality created via language but speaking of a reality 'out there'. The riddle presents a mystery which it then reveals in such a way as to cause a radical surprise in the listener and the reassessment of the listener's world. In this the riddle conveys a transcendent term: that of radically surprising reassessment. Riddles then prefigure creativity in literature.

The riddle first enwraps and then unwraps a secret, a revelation, bringing to light 'a something' hidden in our perception. To reveal, via a riddle, one first needs a secret. *The Gospel*, like a slowly unravelled detective story, is full of secrets, secrets enclosed in the obscurity of paradoxical sayings, prophecies of future times, and parables. The apocalyptic and revelatory nature of the Messianic message shuns the success of mystery, magic and secrecy while shrouded in those very things. Its miracles, designed to open out the esoteric and make it exoteric, open out to the incomprehensibly divine. Secrets and secrecy are at the centre of *The Gospel* as the motivating force of its message; the secret is revealed—as a secret. The prologue starts with a series of secrets for:

> He was in the world, and the world was made by him, and the world knew him not.
> He came unto his own, and his own received him not. (1: 10–11)

And these divine secrets of 'Him' are transferred via this passage into temporal terms, as non-interference; a passivity that never-theless has efficacy as a *sign* in this world. Hence:

> About the midst of the feast Jesus went up into the temple, and taught.
> And the Jews marvelled, saying, How knoweth this man letters, having never learned? (7: 14–15).

As the divine 'secret' working through the temporal is the motivating centre (crisis?) of *The Gospel*, so the riddle is the mechanism whereby communication of the divine message is re-ceived. *The Gospel* is full of riddles, some answered, some not. Hence, of John the Baptist we are told:

> And they asked him, What then? Art thou Elias? And he saith, I am not. Art thou that prophet? And he answered, No.
> Then they said unto him, Who art thou? that we may give an answer to them that sent us. What sayest thou of thyself?
> He said, I *am* the voice of one crying in the wilderness, Make straight the way of the Lord, as said the prophet Esaias. (1: 21–23)

This simple form of riddling question and answer ends itself in a riddle in which John invokes an Old Testament antecedent. And as with Esaias, John says the way must be made 'straight', but for what or for whom? A question is answered with a mystery, a mystery that animates the very question it generates.

John continues the mystery by pointing to Jesus and declaring 'Behold the Lamb of God!' (1: 36). This vitally metaphoric form of statement announces the literal reality as if it were merely figurative. It returns the Baptist's words back to their riddling opening comments but does so by a revelatory movement for John 'points' to Christ. This riddle, in turn, is answered by the disciple who recognises the Lamb as Christ. 'We have' he tells us, 'found the Messias, which is, being interpreted, the Christ'. (1: 41). But this recognition is put in doubt by Nathaniel's riddling reply, formed as a rhetorical question, 'can there any good thing come out of Nazareth?' (1: 46).

After this the riddles become much more complex. Jesus's statements become full of ambiguity and self-contradiction, invoking paradoxes of divine proportion and only half expecting exegesis to unravel them. It is these riddles which retain their obliqueness for the Pharisees to whom ironically Jesus offers the literal truth of his incarnation in the form of a series of riddles that explain themselves even as they pose themselves (as questions to the unbelieving):

> Ye shall seek me, and shall not find *me*: and where I am, *thither* ye cannot come.
> The said the Jews among themselves, Whither will he go, that we shall not find him? will he go unto the dispersed among the Gentiles, and teach the Gentiles?
> What *manner* of saying is this that he said, Ye shall seek me, and shall not find *me*: and where I am, *thither* ye cannot come?
> In the last day, that great *day* of the feast, Jesus stood and cried, saying, If any man thirst, let him come unto me, and drink.
> He that believeth on me, as the scripture hath said, out of his belly shall flow rivers of living water.
> (But this spake he of the Spirit, which they that believe on him should receive: for the Holy Ghost was not yet *given*; because that Jesus was not yet glorified.) (7: 34–39)

This series of enigmas is both obviously open to the believer and stubbornly shut off to the unbeliever. Truth enwraps itself in the language of confusion for:

> Many of the people therefore, when they heard this saying, said, Of a truth this is the Prophet.
> Others said, This is the Christ. But some said, Shall Christ come out of Galilee?
> Hath not the scripture said, That Christ cometh of the seed of David, and out of the town of Bethlehem, where David was?
> So there was a division among the people because of him. (7: 40–43)

Hence, the divine message 'traps' itself as it reveals its presence in temporal language, for temporal language both masks and problematises that divine message, reverses it and de-signifies it.

Following this series of riddles weaker ones follow. One such is the parable of the Good Shepherd. Misunderstood by his disciples Jesus answers his own question in the form of a transcendent metaphor. Christ answers the riddle beyond human understanding. We are told:

> This parable spake Jesus unto them: but they understood not what things they were which he spake unto them.
> Then said Jesus unto them again, Verily, verily, I say unto you, I am the door of the sheep. (10: 6–7)

But this weak riddle is transformed into the complexities of another double riddle: 'And other sheep I have, says Christ, which are not of this fold: them also I must bring, and they shall hear my voice; and there shall be one fold, *and* one shepherd' (10:16). The vitally metaphoric language is itself paradoxically literal, Christ's language of salvation being radically metamorphic.

So strong is the urge of the divine to reveal itself via ambiguity that Christ actually has to explain his method and promise the lucidity of explanation. Having already spoken of the complex relationship he has with the Father, he says, 'a little while, and ye shall not see me: and again, a little while, and yet shall see me, because I go to the Father' (16: 16) He realises that such language is too rich for human consumption. He therefore promises, 'these things have I spoken unto you in proverbs: but the time cometh, when I shall no more speak unto you in proverbs, but I shall shew you plainly of the Father' (16: 25). Indeed, even at his trial Jesus equivocates in the language of riddles; a language that runs through the literature of tragic misunderstanding.

Pilate's nonchalant scepticism completely misunderstands Christ's mission. Pilate's 'What is truth?' is the very question Christ attempts to answer via his riddles and by his enigmatic presence. Pilate, quite simply, misunderstands the nature of the language of semitism: Jesus's concern is precisely with a language cognitive of and revelatory of the 'Truth'. Jesus's special concern with the search for a word explanatory of and synonymous with

Truth (as divinely understood) hinges on his attempt to reveal his Truth, the Truth of *his* presence. This 'new' Truth is, ironically, the oldest Truth, the very essence that generated the Mosaic Law that now *obscures* its origins by its very encoding within the Jewish community.

Beyond the interpretations of the 'verily, verily' speeches of Jesus, Truth or ultimate meaning is the preoccupation of this radical ambiguity. Again and again in *The Gospel* this is the case. Thus:

> He that hath received his testimony hath set to his seal that God is true.
> For he whom God hath sent speaketh the words of God. (3: 33–34)

And:

> I have many things to say and to judge of you: but he that sent me is true; and I speak to the world those things which I have heard of him. (8: 26)

> And ye shall know the truth, and the truth shall make you free.
> They answered him, We be Abraham's seed, and were never in bondage to any man: how sayest thou, Ye shall be made free? (8: 32–33)

Equally, He says, 'I tell you the truth; It is expedient for you that I go away: for if I go not away, the Comforter will not come unto you; but if I depart, I will send him unto you' (16: 7). And finally, 'sanctify them through thy truth: thy word is truth' (17: 17).

However, this desire to express the Truth is enwrapped in ambiguity and secrecy. Even Christ's literal statements are darkly expressive of things *beyond* understanding, and, of course, understanding is needed if Truth is to be recognised.

Indeed, this is why Christ faces a radical problem of expression. How does the divine express itself to the human in terms that the human will comprehend? Christ is aware of the danger of a language that fails to make a unity between concept (language) and object (the world) so that the words expressive of

Truth *are themselves true*, for otherwise the world falls to the
devil and the negation of *Lies*; lies that take over the space
vacated by an unacknowledged Truth. Lies then become a *real*
presence, become *truly* present in the world. Christ recognises
this danger and tells us, 'ye are of *your* father the devil, and the
lusts of your father ye will do. He was a murderer from the beginning, and abode not in the truth, because there is no truth in him.
When he speaketh a lie, he speaketh of his own: for he is a liar,
and the father of it' (8: 44).

Lies speak of that which is *not*, but lies, that absolute
'otherness' of divine language that Christ fears, usurp the space
of Truth and take on the meaning of Truth in the world.
Language becomes the communication of non-communication, a
'murder' of human expressiveness.

Consequently, this need to express the Truth and to connect
language with its ultimate source—literal Truth, from which it
sprang—haunts Christ's purpose. How does one make the divine
and symbolic literal? Christ has to make his relationship to God
explicit, and thus scandalise common sense and common understanding to the point where the latter understands Truth as only
lies:

> He is your God [says Christ] ... if I should say, I know him
> not, I shall be a liar like unto you: but I know him, and keep
> his saying. (8: 54–55)

Christ's statements are at once symbolic and literal: a recognition
of literalness in Christ's language leads to spiritual recognition in
Christ's body. At once His words are enwrapped in metaphor
and transcend metaphor, connecting directly with the object
described: Truth. In this case the object described is usually
Christ himself as Shepherd, Door or Vine. Even when he is
speaking plainly and literally Christ enters into metaphor and
symbolism. The words He uses are attempts by him to make
language concretely real, effective and expressive of the real, to
avoid secrecy and guile by *not* playing on the ambiguity of
language. To do this Christ exploits every ambiguity and guile of
linguistic possibility stretching the credence of the witnesses of
his word to inordinate lengths in an attempt to make the
metaphoric literal. To allay the doubts of his disciples, Christ is

forced to turn the symbolic into the literal via *signs* and *miracles*. By these means Christ tries to convince by *action* those he cannot convince by complex abstract arguments, 'believe me', he says, 'that I *am* in the Father, and the Father in me: or else believe me for the very works' sake' (14:11). Nevertheless, even here Christ, at his most abstract, is most literal. Here Christ literally says what cannot be said: the revelation of his divine relationship with the Father, a speech about the origins of the origin of his speech and about the generation of the literally True.

A further block seems to be placed on the revelation of Truth, a block which is itself, like the use of riddles, integral to *The Gospel*: the use of metaphor. Metaphor is central to the riddles and the narrative. It generates Christ's parables and statements. But to what purpose? How does it function in the text?

Like riddling, metaphoric usage is to do with substituting a known for an unknown proposition, concept or image and then twisting it to show both in a new light. The function of metaphor, so vital to language that one might say language (as substitution for the 'real') is itself metaphor, is one hotly debated.

But in *The Gospel*, metaphor works in this way: a known term and a term to be described make each other visible at the moment the metaphor is expressed, and a transcendent term *incorporating both* is then spontaneously created. *This* term itself, which partakes of the relationship of the known *and* unknown participles of the metaphor, is itself *inexpressible* but, nevertheless, colours the expressive power of the metaphoric phrase. It has efficacy beyond the metaphoric expression such that it can work beyond it but not independently of it. It is generated by the metaphor and yet generates our response to it and to the new reality that it creates. I suggest that this *third unspoken term* is itself creative of reality in that it allows metaphor to manipulate and recreate our world and not merely to describe it. Metaphor, like the riddle, puts the old reality (which is itself invisible through long acquaintance) into a light so strong that that old reality is transcended and replaced. This is a type of law of metaphoric expression: infinite recreation. Thus, when John the Baptist says 'I am the voice of one crying in the wilderness', he removes himself from the world of the humanly expressive into the vehicle of the divinely-told message; a voice without a substance to uphold it. This is far removed from his statements (containing similes) which tell us, 'and John bare record, saying, I saw the Spirit descending from heaven like a dove, and it abode upon him' (1: 32) and is related to the revelation through metaphor of a new reality and a new set of relational spaces, 'and looking upon Jesus as he walked, he saith, Behold the Lamb of God!' (1: 36).

Moreover, Christ turns the metaphoric, through action, into the literal. Thus, the miracle at Cana (expressive of the joining of two terms: the coupling and uniting of oppositions) is the vehicle for the transformation of water, *through* the divine term, into wine:

> And there were set there six waterpots of stone, after the manner of the purifying of the Jews, containing two or three firkins apiece.
>
> Jesus saith unto them, Fill the waterpots with water. And they filled them up to the brim.
>
> And he saith unto them, Draw out now, and bear unto the governor of the feast. And they bare *it*.
>
> When the ruler of the feast had tasted the water that was made wine, and knew not whence it was: (but the servants which drew the water knew;) the governor of the feast called the bridegroom. (2: 6–9)

This metaphor-in-action transfigures and transcends the earthly conditions of reality and transforms that reality as both parable and historical events. It prefigures the transubstantiation of Christ into Spirit at the Resurrection: both metaphoric regeneration and literal regeneration. It literally is at once symbolic of a wider truth and a sign that points directly and emblematically to itself.

When we are given the information: 'Now Jacob's well was there. Jesus therefore, being wearied with *his* journey, sat thus on the well: *and* it was about the sixth hour' (4: 6) we see, quite clearly, that here the metaphor is triggered by the emphasis on the italicised *his*, the fulcrum of the metaphorical change from mundane reality into a literal, yet also symbolic, language, dealing with life's travail.

But the most sustained and wide use of metaphor in action is the metaphorical use of bread and wine—at once flesh and blood:

> Then Jesus said unto them, Verily, verily, I say unto you, Moses gave you not that bread from heaven; but my Father giveth you the true bread from heaven.
> For the bread of God is he which cometh down from heaven, and giveth life unto the world. (6: 32–33)

> I am that bread of life. (6: 48)

> I am the living bread which came down from heaven: if any man eat of this bread, he shall live for ever: and the bread that I will give is my flesh, which I will give for the life of the world.
> The Jews therefore strove among themselves, saying, How can this man give us *his* flesh to eat? (6: 51–52)

> Whoso eateth my flesh, and drinketh my blood, hath eternal life; and I will raise him up at the last day. (6: 54)

The Jews, represented here as sceptics, fall into a complex paradox. How, they ask, can one eat of a real man's flesh and drink a real man's blood? This, their question implies, is *literally* ridiculous and indeed abominable. Surely the statement is symbolic? But Christ's statement is unambiguous and literal. Christ states the literal as a scandal of language. What he says he means, not symbolically but literally. Hence, Christ's metaphor is literal from one side and Christ's literalness metaphoric from another. Christ's words are literally metaphoric creating a new literalness through the use of metaphor. The Jews cannot see the literalness of Christ's statement—a literalness that transcends the created world of flesh and death. Christ's flesh is of another order as the 'manna' which sustained body and soul. *'His'* flesh, ask the sceptics, what's special about his flesh? Christ's flesh is the transcendent meat of the soul, a meal for spirit. Hence, Christ is being literally and radically ambiguous in his straightforward *unparadoxical* statement of *fact*.

Let us turn to the last complex metaphoric usage I wish to speak of, at least for the moment:

Believest thou not that I am in the Father, and the Father in me? the words that I speak unto you I speak not of myself: but the Father that dwelleth in me, he doeth the works.

Believe me that I *am* in the Father, and the Father in me: or else believe me for the very works' sake. (14:10–11)

Here expressively, the one term is found in the other and while Christ continually points to God's transcendence, the double terminology of the father in the son, the son in the father, ends in the vision of the two combined, such that the ultimate term transcends both. Thus, 'God *is* a Spirit: and they that worship him must worship *him* in spirit and in truth' (4: 24). This last, again enwraps the believer in a mystery which is unrevealable except through the metaphoric relationship of known and unknown just described.

Thus we see that, via riddles and metaphors, Christ attempts to express a transcendent reality beyond the known, now incarnate in the events narrated, via a text which attempts to unite with the Truth of which it speaks and stand thereby outside history or textuality or any history of a literature. The text directs the world through its language, it poses outside the world as divine *intervention*; incarnate in a temporality which initiates Christian action. The divine Word revealed, and yet incarnate in the Bible's text, becomes not another object for textual exercise, but instead a form of *action*, of event, of a staging and placing and directing and coming together. *The Gospel's* language takes upon itself a certain cryptic movement, an opening of its own language as if language had an inside and an outside and here the outside slowly turned itself inward revealing its innermost essence, making manifest its hidden and divine power. This is action, for it directs the reader (as a recognition *within* the reader) and brings the reader to God.

We have seen that through the radical ambiguity of riddles and metaphors at once literal and symbolic, plain and complex, lucid yet dark, the 'message' of Christ is conveyed. We have further seen that by this method a series of transcendent terms has been generated in which the old order is recreated and regenerated via the Christian message. One way of completing this removal of the old ways is via Christ's statements which play backward and forward in time—time as pre-existent *and all present at one moment*. The other is via a series of miracles or signs that rend the veil of human reality to show a glimpse of a transcendent *co-existent* reality into which occasionally, via the divine, one may pass. In this co-existent reality, natural reality (the reality of our world) is overturned.

The next stage after riddles and metaphors is then the series of signs and words which overturn the order of nature and culture. We have already seen Christ turn water to wine, and the story of the loaves and fishes needs no retelling. Nevertheless, Christ overturns the natural order wherever possible to place himself and that *other* order in perspective as it is incarnate in *this world now*. That other order is *here* but *absent*, expressed through the actions of this world and thus accorded the status of a wonder. Hence, 'but he saith unto them, It is I; be not afraid' (6: 20) or when he overturns the order of culture:

> Therefore they gathered *them* together, and filled twelve baskets with the fragments of the five barley loaves, which remained over and above unto them that had eaten.
> Then those men, when they had seen the miracle that Jesus did, said, This is of a truth that prophet that should come into the world. (6: 13–14)

But, more importantly, Christ overturns the natural human conditions of birth and death, redefining death as *rebirth*. Here, Christ's most definite statements on the transcending of the older order are via statements about mortality:

> Verily, verily, I say unto you, If a man keep my saying, he shall never see death. (8: 51)

> Jesus said unto her, I am the resurrection and the life: he that believeth in me, though he were dead, yet shall he live. (11: 25)

The raising of Lazarus is given extra emphasis by the naturalism of, 'Jesus said, Take ye away the stone. Martha, the sister of him that was dead, saith unto him, Lord, by this time he stinketh: for he hath been *dead* four days' (11: 39), which goes before the supernaturalism of:

> Then they took away the stone *from the place* where the dead was laid. And Jesus lifted up *his* eyes, and said, Father, I thank thee that thou hast heard me.
>
> And I knew that thou hearest me always: but because of the people which stand by I said *it*, that they may believe that thou has sent me.
>
> And when he thus had spoken, he cried with a loud voice, Lazarus, come forth.
>
> And he that was dead came forth, bound hand and foot with graveclothes: and his face was bound about with a napkin. Jesus saith unto them, Loose him, and let him go. (11: 41–44)

Evidently, all this presages the resurrection of Christ himself in which the divine *returns* to this *world* to give proof precisely of its departing from it.

But above the laws of nature are the laws of men—the laws of men in their covenant with God. The divine order prescribed in the Torah and given through Moses to the Israelites transcends natural order via its convenant with the Almighty. This law governs not only the relationship of man to man but of man to God. Indeed, it is this law that supposedly has a divine origin, dwelling with God and coming down to man, that sets man apart and that sets the chosen people apart who wear the mark of the covenant on their penis via circumcision and pass on that covenant by the act of generation via their seed. Christ offends most by transgressing that covenant and that law. It is his over-turning of this order that is most serious.

The law is mentioned a great many times in *The Gospel* especially when,

> Philip findeth Nathanael, and saith unto him, We have found him, of whom Moses in the law, and the prophets, did write, Jesus of Nazareth, the son of Joseph. (1: 45)

and when .Christ says,

Did not Moses give you the law, and *yet* none of you keepeth the law? Why go ye about to kill me? (7: 19)

Christ is a breaker of these laws and is mocked as a judge:

They say unto him, Master, this woman was taken in adultery, in the very act.

Now Moses in the law commanded us, that such should be stoned: but what sayest thou?

This they said, tempting him, that they might have to accuse him. But Jesus stooped down, and with *his* finger wrote on the ground, *as though he heard them not.*

So when they continued asking him, he lifted up himself, and said unto them, He that is without sin among you, let him first cast a stone at her.

And again he stooped down, and wrote on the ground.

And they which heard *it*, being convicted by *their own* conscience, went out one by one, beginning at the eldest, *even* unto the last: and Jesus was left alone, and the woman standing in the midst. (8: 4–9)

Nevertheless, the law proposed by Christ is meant to transcend the very law of the Jews, and in so doing declare Christ's pre-existent divine nature. He tells the Jews: 'ye are from beneath; I am from above: ye are of this world; I am not of this world' (8: 32). Consequently Christ talks of the divine order and covenant, saying:

Moses therefore gave unto you circumcision; (not because it is of Moses, but of the fathers;) and ye on the sabbath day circumcise a man.

If a man on the sabbath day receive circumcision, that law of Moses should not be broken; are ye angry at me, because I have made a man every whit whole on the sabbath day? (7: 22–23)

and by so doing issues new commandments, 'this is my commandment, That ye love one another, as I have loved you' (15: 12). Divine order as natural order *and spirit* overthrows merely natural generation and prepares for *regeneration*:

Jesus answered and said unto him, Verily, verily, I say unto thee, Except a man be born again, he cannot see the kingdom of God.

Nicodemus saith unto him, How can a man be born when he is old? can he enter the second time into his mother's womb, and be born?

Jesus answered, Verily, verily, I say unto thee, Except a man be born of water and *of* the Spirit, he cannot enter into the kingdom of God.

That which is born of the flesh is flesh; and that which is born of the Spirit is spirit.

Marvel not that I said unto thee, Ye must be born again. (3: 3–7)

In *Genesis* it is the seed that gives birth and passes on the law via the covenant:

And God said unto Abraham, Thou shalt keep my covenant therefore, thou, and thy seed after thee in their generations.

This *is* my covenant, which ye shall keep, between me and you and thy seed after thee; Every man child among you shall be circumcised. (Gen.17: 9–10)

In *The Gospel* this has become regeneration via the synonyms of seed: 'bread' and 'water', 'blood' and 'wine', changing and transmuting the divinely given covenant of duty to the *law* via *sexual* generation into duty to the divine Christian message in *oneself* via *spiritual* regeneration through the 'body' and the 'word'. Accusation, condemnation, punishment and salvation all participate in the court of the divine law with Christ placed between the 'new' law and humanity as humanity's advocate.

Before turning to the wider implications of this overturning, and transcendence via metaphor and riddle, I should like to look at the idea of witnesses in the text. The witness is a key figure in *The Gospel*, both accusatory (as the Pharisees) or defensive (as the disciples). The witness must be there to *see* and *hear* the signs, for, 'then said Jesus unto him, Except ye see signs and wonders, ye will not believe' (4: 48). Christ's message must have an addressee and is therefore *always* open to misinterpretation. The witnesses from John the Baptist's:

> The same came for a witness, to bear witness of the Light, that all *men* through him might believe.
> He was not that Light, but *was sent* to bear witness of that Light. (1: 7–18)

to Christ's:

> Our fathers did eat manna in the desert; as it is written, He gave them bread from heaven to eat. ... Verily, verily, I say unto you, Moses gave you not that bread from heaven; but my Father giveth you the true bread from heaven. (6: 31–32)

bear witness to the signs and works. The blind man is made to see, *himself* an incarnation of the signs of a new order, as witness the blind man who now literally sees the light. The final witness is 'the disciple which testifieth of these things, and wrote of these things' (21: 24).

How then does the witness function in *The Gospel*? Each witness is required to see or hear a divine 'presence', a putting forth into the world of divinity—he does not see or hear the divine directly but only its representations.

I have said that the Old Testament covenant is sealed on the penis of its witnesses: Abraham and his family and descendants. Christ ordains a new covenant via the *seal of* the bread and water. As the Torah was manna, so manna (bread) becomes the body of Christ. Both covenants are passed on first by generation via the seed and secondly by regeneration via bread and baptismal water. Abraham's descendant Moses reveals the Mosaic law as operative long before its revelation to the people of Israel. Christ reveals His order of love and Grace as also operative long before its revelation.

Both laws are revealed to selected witnesses who will pass on the message via generation. These witnesses are integral to the signs they witness, participating in them and becoming part of them—they are required by the signs to offer those signs significance. The semination of the witnesses' descendants through the seed leads to dissemination of the witnesses' words via speech, each witness pointing beyond himself to the divine order.

The witnesses find that words animate them, recreating the world for them in a series of meanings transmitted through the image and concept of birth. We have already 'heard' Christ's answer to Nicodemus (3: 3–7) but he also tells us:

> A woman when she is in travail hath sorrow, because her hour is come: but as soon as she is delivered of the child, she remembereth no more the anguish, for joy that a man is born into the world. (16: 21)

Or, again, using synonyms for birth, He says, 'I sent you to reap that whereon ye bestowed no labour: other men laboured, and ye are entered into their labours (4: 38).[3]

The 'Torah' and the 'Trinity', their origins prehistorically female, go out as divine 'spermaticos logos'.[4]

Yet, these ideas of a divinely emanating word-seed, generative of revelation within the witnesses, does not go far enough in explaining *The Gospel's* own textual power and that textual power's relationship to its witnesses both within and outside the text. This is where I shall now turn—to *The Gospel's* theory of divine textuality and divine authorship.

I said at the beginning that *The Gospel* is a myth not only of creation but of creative power wrapped in divine law and the divine Word. I refer specifically to the creative role of 'The Word' in *The Gospel* and its exposition in the prologue.

In what way then does the prologue express the presence of the Word and explain, if it can, the workings of the Word? We are told:

> In the beginning was the Word, and the Word was with God, and the Word was God. (1: 1)

The Gospel opens with a statement of supreme lucidity and ultimate literalness and, yet, it is ambiguous and secretive and mysterious. What indeed is this Word, that is pre-existent and that is not merely with God but *is* God. This is a real difficulty expressed as it is in a riddle: the ultimate riddle of the origins of existence expressed abstractly and philosophically. As *Genesis* deals with material generation so *The Gospel* deals with the abstract regeneration of living substance and living men.

The translators of the *King James Bible* chose the idea of Word for Logos and in doing so created a mysterious and silent speech within the speech of man. For Logos not only is the principle of rational being but is animating spirit and breath too. As air in motion, spirit equals expression.[5] Not from man but from God this divinely creative Word brings history and the cosmos into existence. Via its presence it bestows life, animation, breath and the capacity to understand its presence in the universe. The Word is a divine presence and an abstraction without substance. Its status is ultimate and endless and it creates without being created and it creates the cosmos as a text in which divine purpose is displayed through meaning. The Word is the animating principle of the Bible's symbolism and is itself an ultimate symbol. However, as Jung points out, such an archetypal predisposing function as the Word is its own negation. Forever absent, it has presence *only* in its incarnation, in those things it has created. Its presence is always deferred through creation, for it lies beyond and behind creation as its very animating principle. Thus, the Word animates its own elucidation without becoming present. Moreover, light and life become one only to become dark again in the mystery of the Word. It can be evoked and invoked but not *expressed*. Like the name of God it is impossible to pronounce. In such a way the centre of the text as well as its beginning and its ultimate meaning always delay presence as an always expected revelation—an idea quite out of harmony with the manifest message of *The Gospel* itself.

Moreover, the Word is itself under a constraint, a compulsion to create, under a law that is beyond the Word itself acting upon it as its *Fate*. And yet this fate is contained in the Word (the Logos) itself. Indeed, this Word has its roots in the Torah and the feminine principle behind the Jewish law—a principle now become law as masculine 'seed'.[6] Thus, the Kosmos, God as lawgiver, puts forth the Word which is non-historical but makes sense of the historical; the spermaticos logos creates temporal time and thereby creates, as time's negation, the idea in man of the non-temporal (the divine). Man thereby finds God.[7]

This Word is independent of human volition—it *speaks man* but cannot be spoken by him. The voice is possessed by a message it cannot constrain. The voice becomes an instrument of daemonic force, a vehicle and a vessel of the divine. Hence, John becomes the vehicle of its pronouncements and demons recognise its presence. In *The Gospel according to St. Mark* we are told of the demon that fled from Christ's voice:

> And they were astonished at his doctrine: for he taught them as one that had authority, and not as the scribes.
>
> And there was in their synagogue a man with an unclean spirit; and he cried out,
>
> Saying, Let *us* alone; what have we to do with thee, thou Jesus of Nazareth? art thou come to destroy us? I know thee who thou art, the Holy One of God.
>
> And Jesus rebuked him, saying, Hold thy peace, and come out of him.
>
> And when the unclean spirit had torn him, and cried with a loud voice, he came out of him. (*Mark* 1: 22–26)

While in *Acts* the disciples are possessed by it as it descends through the mediation of the Holy Ghost.

Indeed, the Word is the very animating principle of the meaning of the cosmos and its laws. As such it has the power to regenerate. In *The Gospel* Jesus heals the blind man:

> And as *Jesus* passed by, he saw a man which was blind from *his* birth.
>
> And his disciples asked him, saying, Master, who did sin, this man, or his parents, that he was born blind?
>
> Jesus answered, Neither hath this man sinned, nor his parents: but that the works of God should be made manifest to him.
>
> I must work the works of him that sent me, while it is day: the night cometh, when no man can work.
>
> As long as I am in the world, I am the light of the world.
>
> When he had thus spoken, he spat on the ground, and made clay of the spittle, and he annointed the eyes of the blind man with the clay,
>
> And said unto him, Go, wash in the pool of Siloam, (which is by interpretation, Sent.) He went his way therefore, and washed, and came seeing. (9: 1–7)

In so doing he completes the circular movement of the Word. By the use of clay and spittle we find Jesus invokes the following sequence: The Word = light = life = breath(spittle) = light = life = Word. The divine tautology is then complete.

But this movement is not simply circular. Its immense tautological thrust is, at the same time, linear. The Word goes out but does not end in a void, Hence, God says, 'so shall my word be that goeth forth out of my mouth: it shall not return unto me void, but it shall accomplish that which I please, and it shall prosper *in the thing* whereto I sent it' (*Isaiah* 55: 11). The Word, as the potential force of creation, points through creation and brings creation into existence in its passage. The Word looks forward to its self-recovery at the end of history. The beginning and the end are both present in the Word. At the end of history and at the beginning of time the Word is meaningless. Only in its incarnation, that is, as other than itself, as other than its 'true' nature, can the Word have power. The word speaks as an uncanny repetition of the Word *in* time by speaking from beyond time—beyond the grave for, 'then they took away the stone *from the place* where the dead was laid. And Jesus lifted up *his* eyes, and said, Father, I thank thee that thou hast heard me' (*The Gospel* 11: 41). Even here the Word speaks from the grave and into incarnation in time—the time of its living auditors.

The Word is incarnate in words which witness its presence as the witnesses acknowledge Christ's signs. While it points to its own invisibility as Truth or ultimate meaning the Word, nevertheless, generates a text of words in which it finds an embodiment that is silent and unnamable. The Bible with its special status becomes a very special text; a text concerned with the invisibility of this Word, this Logos of creativity. Thus, the Bible shows us the Word moving from outside time into time, into its textual representative such that the transcendent term is actually incarnate in the essence of those representatives: that is, they represent nothing but themselves. However, in so doing, they stand a witness to *the message*, for, 'there are also many other things which Jesus did, the which, if they should be written every one, I suppose that even the world itself could not contain the books that should be written. Amen' (21: 25). Each witness becomes a participant and the message is recreated each time it is invoked, each time we as readers invoke the signs of *The Book*. Thus, we too are pre-empted by this book—born into its structure via our religious upbringing and culture. The Book places the reader in the position of seeker in the act of recreating the past as an urgent event in our present. It demands we fathom the mystery of the message, this urgent silent, open secret.

The Book stands as a *memorial* to the events it describes, itself a witness, through the gift of the Holy Ghost, which as it descends appears to be nothing less than the *gift of memory*:

> When therefore he was risen from the dead, his disciples remembered that he had said this unto them; and they believed the scripture, and the word which Jesus had said. (2: 22)

> But the Comforter, *which is* the Holy Ghost, whom the Father will send in my name, he shall teach you all things, and bring all things to your remembrance, whatsoever I have said unto you. (14: 26)

The Book influences the Text of God's message and we witness the text of the Book in which that message is incarnate.

The ultimate concern of the Word is encapsulated within the reader in his or her quest to find out the mystery in their own heart. The Book desires itself to be both exterior and interior text, a *text which speaks through its witnesses as part of its efficacy*. By re-reading itself through the reader it re-interprets the reader's position and definition in the world.[8] The Book becomes a repository of cultural and individual *memory*: a remembrance of the divine; a memory locked together with the Word.

The Book is rewritten on the body of the desciple, it anticipates and directs the disciple to it and beyond to the interior dialogue of individual memory and the divine remembrance. Temporal memory is thus linked through this text to a memory of spirituality outside temporal history. The disciple is 'forced' to read an interior text, the text of his 'heart', in which the Christian gospel now is to be found. The Bible both surrounds the disciple with textuality and becomes the essence of the disciple. The language it expresses finally becomes that very thing the Word stands for in proxy—divine *silence*.

I am suggesting a difficulty: namely, that at the heart of this text there is a meaning which is forever silent, at once rationally deferred—non-spoken impossible to name—, and yet, through its representations, always present within them and speaking out of them. In *The Gospel according to St. John* the author or authors tried to express a mystery, that of communication itself, in a divine and historical text, a text that attempts to explain the divine and its intervention on earth. Those authors tried to communicate the paradoxical presence of a divine but literal term and a transcendent secret. They talk of lucidity, clarity, truth, in the ambiguous terms of convolution, equivocation and circumlocution. By pointing directly at Truth they point away from it and surround it *in* riddles. The text invokes that of which it cannot speak while it speaks through its interlocutors with divine ventriloquism.

This transcendent term finds its place only in its incarnation. It speaks via secrets, riddles, parables and metaphors. Like the story of the Marriage at Cana, in which metaphor had efficacy in the world via its third unnamable but creative term (creating wine out of water), so *The Gospel* proposes that the text predisposes its reader, positions him as witness, and converts him into a vehicle. The text controls the reader and the reader is controlled by such a text. Even a refusal is a form of controlled reaction.

This text is compulsive and daemonic. It possesses its reader as a text written by men (or written by God?) to explain the presence of divinity.

The Word confounds its analysis for it is *embodied* in that analysis as the very possibility of analysis itself; an analysis that cannot understand its own origin, its own compulsion to read. The Word recognises itself *through* its mediator the Book, and the human reader of the Book. The Bible 're-reads' the reader in as much as it *reinterprets* the reader's spiritual position. The Word is in the Book but *not* of it. The Word is in the reading but not of it. But the Word is not always absenting itself behind its representatives for those representatives give it a presence on the level of another spatial and temporal plain—on the level of the miraculous—coterminous with, but hidden in, the unexplored and *transcendent relationship* between the words we read and the phrases we construct. Paradoxically the plenitude of our linguistic system hides the poverty of the Word. Our rich tongues hide naked Truth in the act of naming it.

Notes

Chapter One

1. John Donne, *The Complete English Poems*, ed., A. J. Smith (Hamondsworth: Penguin, 1981), p. 58.
2. William Shakespeare. *The Complete Works*, ed., W. J. Craig (London: Oxford University Press, 1969), pp. 1108-9.

   I have chosen this particular printing of the sonnet because it includes a hyphen. Many editors chose to leave this out and in so doing leave a type of spacing of the 'unsaid'. This rendering of the sonnet makes visible the 'invisible' space between 'master' and 'mistress' and allows us to speculate on the graphics that generate relational spaces from which 'meaning' is read off. The hyphenated rendering is, actually, more crude than the implicit non-hyphenated printings, making obvious what is merely implied, restricting our interpretation even as it generates it.
3. Adrienne Rich, *On Lies, Secrets and Silence* (London: Virago, 1980).

Chapter Two

1. This edition: Jane Austen, *Mansfield Park*, ed., Tony Tanner (Harmondsworth: Penguin, 1983).
2. Avrom Fleishman, *A Reading of Mansfield Park*, (Minneapolis: University of Minnesota, 1967), p. 47.
3. *Ibid.*, p. 67.
4. *Ibid.*, pp. 62-3.
5. *Ibid.*, p. 63.
6. *Ibid.*, p. 67.
7. *Ibid.*, p. 63.
8. R. D. Laing, *The Facts of Life* (Harmondsworth: Penguin, 1979), p. 62.

Chapter Three

1. See Peter Gay, *Freud, Jews and Other Germans* (Oxford: Oxford University Press, 1978), p. 36.
2. Sigmund Freud, 'Address Delivered at the Goethe House at Frankfurt', [1930], *Standard Edition of the Complete Works of Sigmund Freud,* (SE) trans. James Strachey, Vol. 1-24, Vol. 21 (London: Hogarth, 1955), pp. 208-12 (p. 211).
3. Marie Bonaparte, *The Life and Works of Edgar Allan Poe* trans. James Strachey (London: Hogarth Press, 1971). p. 624.
4. *Ibid.*, p. 597.
5. Harold Bloom, *The Anxiety of Influence* (New York: Oxford University Press, 1973), p. 14.
6. Bonaparte, *op.cit.*, p. 631.
7. *Ibid.*
8. *Ibid.*
9. *Ibid.*
10. *Ibid.*
11. *Ibid.*
12. *Ibid.*, p. 597.
13. *Ibid.*
14. *Ibid.*
15. *Ibid.*
16. *Ibid.*, p. 639.
17. André Green, *The Tragic Effect* tr. Alan Sheridan (Cambridge: Cambridge University Press, 1979), p. 10.
18. Bonaparte, *op.cit.*, p. 643.
19. Philip Rieff, *Freud: The Mind of the Moralist* (Chicago: Chicago University Press, 1979), p. 8.
20. Bonaparte, *op.cit.*, p. 636.
21. Anthony Wilden, *System and Structure* (London: Tavistock, 1981) p. xli.
22. Bonaparte, *op.cit.*, p. 643.
23. *Ibid.*, p. 662.
24. *Ibid.*, p. 649.
25. Bloom, *op.cit.*, p. 15.
26. Sigmund Freud, 'Psychoanalytic Notes on an Autobiographical Account of a Case of Paranoia ("Schreber")', [1910], *SE*, Vol. 12, pp. 9-80 (p. 147).
27. Bonaparte, *op.cit.*, p. 639.
28. *Ibid.*, p. 622.
29. Wilden, *op.cit.*, p. 67.
30. Wolfgang Iser, 'The Current Situation of Literary Theory: Key Concepts and the Imaginary', *New Literary History* (1979), 1-20 (p. 7).
31. Bonaparte, *op.cit.*, p. 650.
32. *Ibid.* See also Sigmund Freud, 'Character and Anal Eroticism', [1908], *SE*, Vol. 9, pp. 169-75 (p. 174), Freud writes: 'In reality, wherever archaic modes of thought have predominated or persist—in the ancient civilizations, in myths, fairy tales and superstitions, in unconcious

thinking, in dreams and neurosis — money is brought into the most intimate relationship with dirt. We know that the gold which the devil gives his paramours turns into excrement after his departure, and the devil is certainly nothing else than the personification of the repressed unconscious instinctual life'.

33. Quoted by Wolf Mankowitz, *The Extraordinary Mr Poe* (London: Weidenfeld and Nicolson, 1978), p. 105.
34. John Carlos Rowe, 'Writing and Truth in Poe's "Narrative of A. Gordon Pym"', *Glyph* (1977), p. 105.
35. Edgar Allan Poe, 'Ligeia', *Virginia Edition of the Complete Works of Edgar Allan Poe*, (*VE*) ed. James A. Harrison, Vols. 1-27, Vol. 2 (New York: AMS Press Inc., 1965), pp. 248-68 (p. 248).
36. Poe, 'The Man that was Used Up', *VE*, Vol. 3, pp. 259-72 (p. 259).
37. Poe, 'Ligeia', p. 248.
38. Poe, 'The Man that was Used Up', p. 259.
39. Poe, 'Ligeia', p. 248.
40. Poe, 'The Man that was Used Up', pp. 259-60.
41. *Ibid.*, pp. 269-271.
42. *Ibid.*, p. 259.
43. Bonaparte, *op.cit.*, p. 633. See also Aldous Huxley, 'Vulgarity in Literature in *Poe: a Collection of Critical Essays* ed. Robert Regan (New Jersey: Prentice-Hall, 1967), pp. 31-7.
44. Harry Levin, *The Power of Blackness* (London: Faber and Faber, 1958), p. 105.
45. Bonaparte, p. 633.
46. Michel Foucault, *Language, Counter-Memory, Practice*, trans. D. F. Bouchard and S. Simon, ed. D. F. Bouchard. (Ithaca: Coppell University Press, 1977), p. 64.
47. Bonaparte, *op.cit.*, p. 598.
48. *Ibid.*, p. 649.
49. *Ibid.*, p. 596.
50. *Ibid.*, p.598.
51. *Ibid.*, p.654.
52. *Ibid.*
53. R. D. Laing, *The Divided Self* (Harmondsworth: Penguin, 1965), p. 102.
54. *Ibid.*, p. 100.
55. Bonaparte, *op.cit.*, p. 654.
56. Sandor Ferenczi, 'Introjection and Transference', trans. Ernest Jones, in *Contributions to Psycho-Analysis* (Boston: Gorham Press, 1916), pp. 30-79 (p. 71).
57. *Ibid.*, p. 71.
58. Jacques Lacan 'Seminar on "The Purloined Letter"', trans. Jeffrey Mehlman *Yale French Studies*, (1973), pp. 38-72 (p. 47).
59. Rieff, *op.cit.*, p. 87.
60. Poe, 'The Facts in the Case of M. Valdemar', *VE*, Vol. 6, pp. 154-66 (p. 155).
61. *Ibid.*, p. 154.
62. *Ibid.*, pp. 154-5.

63. *Ibid.*, p. 155.
64. *Ibid.*
65. *Ibid.*
66. *Ibid.*, p. 156.
67. *Ibid.*, p. 158.
68. *Ibid.*, p. 159.
69. *Ibid.*, p. 162.
70. *Ibid.*
71. *Ibid.*, pp. 162-3.
72. *Ibid.*, p. 163.
73. Roland Barthes, 'Textual Analysis of Poe's "Valdemar"' trans. Geoff Bennington in *Untying the Text*, ed. Robert Young (Boston: Routledge and Kegan Paul, 1981), pp. 135-61 (p. 153).
74. Poe, *VE*, Vol. 6, p. 163.
75. *Ibid.*, p. 164.
76. *Ibid.*
77. *Ibid.*, p. 165.
78. *Ibid.*
79. *Ibid.*, p. 166.
80. *Ibid.*, p. 157.
81. *Ibid.*, p. 166.
82. *Ibid*;
83. Green, *op.cit.*, p. 18.
84. Sigmund Freud and Joseph Breuer, 'Studies on Hysteria', [1895], *SE*, Vol. 2, pp. 1-319 (p. 193).
85. Sigmund Freud, 'Inhibitions, Symptoms and Anxiety', [1925], *SE*, Vol. 20, pp. 87-169 (p. 125).

Chapter Four

1. Quoted in Glynne Wickham, *Early English Stages 1300 to 1660* Vol. 2, Pt. 1 (London: Routledge and Kegan Paul, 1963) pp. 86-7.
2. *Ibid.*, p. 77.
3. *Ibid.*, p. 82.
4. See Susan Sonntag, *Illness as Metaphor* (Harmondsworth: Penguin, 1979).
5. Antonin Artaud, 'Theatre and the Plague' in *The Theatre and its Double* trans. Victor Corti (London: Calder and Boyers, 1974), pp. 7-22.
6. *Ibid.*, p. 7.
7. *Ibid.*, p. 8.
8. *Ibid.*, p. 9.
9. *Ibid.*, p. 10.
10. *Ibid.*, p. 11.
11. *Ibid.*
12. Franz Kafka, 'In the Penal Settlement' in *Metamorphosis and Other Stories* trans. Willa and Edwin Muir (Harmondsworth: Penguin, 1978), pp. 167-200 (pp. 173-80).

13. Artaud, *loc.cit.*, p.11.
14. *Ibid.*, p. 12.
15. *Ibid.*, p. 15.
16. *Ibid.*,p. 22.
17. *Ibid.*, pp. 21 and 20.

Chapter Five

1. Ed., Carolyn Ruth Swift Lenz, Gayle Green, Carol Thomas Nealy, *The Woman's Part: Feminist Criticism of Shakespeare* (Urbana: University of Illinois Press, 1980), p. 6. See also Elizabeth Sacks, *Shakespeare's Imagery of Pregnancy* (New York: St. Martin's Press, 1980).
2. Paula S. Borggen, 'Female Sexuality as Power in Shakespeare's Plays' in *The Women's Part, op.cit.*, p. 18.
3. Lisa Jardine, *Still Harping on Daughters* (Brighton: Harvester Press, 1983), pp. 7 and 10.
4. Jardine points out the equation of silence with virtue and articulateness with vice and disorder in the concept of womanliness at this time. *Ibid.*, pp. 57-8.
5. Kathleen Raine, *Yeats, the Tarot and the Golden Dawn* (Dublin: Dolmen Press, 1972). Raine points out the Fool's equivalence in the occult and tarot with zero and quotes Aleister Crowley's comment on the Fool in tarot pack as the 'initial nothing' (p. 18).
6. Jardine, *op.cit.*, p. 19.
7. *Ibid.*, p. 93.
8. Angela Carter, *The Sadeian Woman* (London: Virago, 1979), p. 7.
9. Jardine, *op.cit.*, p. 110.
10. George Steiner, *Language and Silence* (London: Faber and Faber, 1967), p. 228.

Chapter Seven

1. Gabriel Josipovici, *The World and The Book* (London: Macmillan, 1971), p.29.
2. *Ibid.*, p. 30.
3. *Ibid.*, p. 29.
4. *Ibid.*, p. 30.
5. *Ibid.*, p. 37.
6. Isidore Epstein, *Judaism* (London: Pelican, 1982), p. 240.
7. Josipovici, *op.cit*, pp. 26 and 32.
8. Poe, *Eureka* in *VE* Vol. 16, pp. 179-315 (p. 214).
9. Frances Yates, *The Rosicrucian Enlightenment* (London: Routledge and Kegan Paul, 1972), p. 98.
10. Frances Yates, *The Art of Memory* (Harmondsworth: Penguin, 1966), P. 22.

11. Jacques Derrida, 'Freud and the Scene of Writing' in *Writing and Difference* trans. Alan Bass (London: Routledge and Kegan Paul, 1978), pp. 196-231 (p. 224).
12. Sigmund Freud quoted in Derrida, *loc.cit.*, p. 223.
13. *Ibid.*, p. 226.
14. *Ibid.*
15. *Ibid.*, p. 227.
16. *Ibid.*
17. R. D. Laing, *The Voice of Experience* (Harmondsworth: Penguin, 1982,) p. 158.

Chapter Eight

1. See C. K. Barrett, *The Gospel according to St. John* (London: SPCK Press, 1978), p. 31. See also W. F. Howard, *Christianity according to St. John* (London: Duckworth, 1943), p. 26.
2. J. C. Fenton, *The Gospel according to St. John in the RSV* (Oxford: Clarendon Press, 1970), p. 21.
3. See W. F. Howard, *The Fourth Gospel in Recent Criticism and Interpretation* (London: Epworth Press, 1945), p.203.
4. See Joseph Campbell, *The Masks of God* (Harmondsworth: Penguin, 1976), p.108.
5. George Johnston, *The Spirit-Paraclete in the Gospel according to St. John* (Cambridge: Cambridge University Press, 1970), p.3.
6. See Howard, *op.cit.* See also Eduard Lohse, *The New Testament Environment* trans. John Seely (London: SCM Press, 1980), p. 167.
7. E. C. Hoskyns quoted by A. M. Hunter, *According to St. John* (London: SCM Press, 1975), p.1.
8. Eduard Lohse, *op.cit.*, p.256.

Acknowledgement

The author and publisher are grateful to The Hogarth Press and the estate of Marie Bonaparte for permission to reprint extracts from *The Life and Work of Edgar Allan Poe.*

Index

The Author:

CLIVE BLOOM is currently Co-ordinator for American Studies at Middlesex Polytechnic. His interests range widely across literature, psychology and theology and he is keen to promote the study of forgotten or neglected writings and cultural practices. Clive Bloom is General Editor of the series *Insights* (Macmillan) concerned with literature and popular culture.